Housesteads Crags from Cuddy's Crags

HADRIAN'S WALL PATH

The Hadrian's Wall Path is an official National Trail that follows the 84-mile (135km) length of Hadrian's Wall between Bowness-on-Solway in the west and Wallsend in Newcastle upon Tyne. The trail typically takes a week to walk, and is suitable for walkers and trekkers at all levels of experience.

Contents and using this guide

This booklet of Ordnance Survey 1:25,000 Explorer maps has been designed for convenient use on the trail and includes:

- a key to map pages (pages 2–3) showing where to find the maps for each stage.
- the full and up-to-date line of the National Trail (in several places the route has evolved and not yet been updated on the underlying Explorer map), designed for use eastbound or westbound and including an extension to the east coast at South Shields.
- an extract from the OS Explorer map legend (pages 52–54).

In addition, the *Walking Hadrian's Wall Path* guidebook describes the full route in both directions with lots of other practical and historical information.

© Cicerone Press 2023
Second edition 2023
ISBN-13: 978 1 7863 1151 1
First edition 2015

Photos © Mark Richards 2015
© Crown copyright and database rights 2015 OS PU100012932

Key to map pages

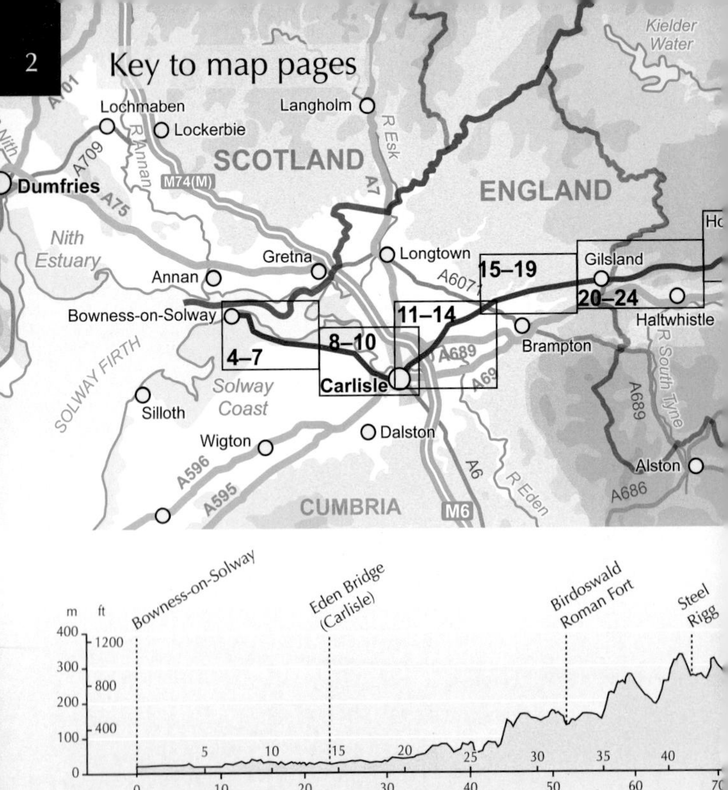

HADRIAN'S WALL PATH

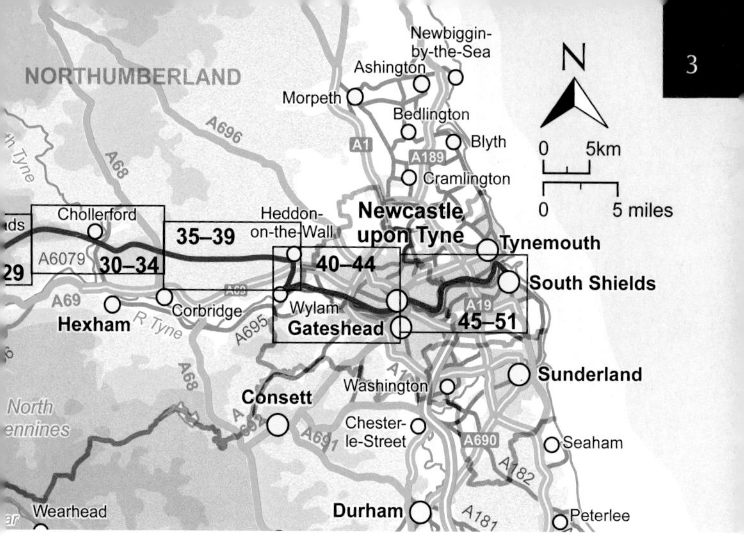

NORTHUMBERLAND
Newbiggin-by-the-Sea
Ashington
Morpeth
Bedlington
Blyth
Cramlington
A696
A68
A1
A189
N
0 5km
0 5 miles
Chollerford
Heddon-on-the-Wall
Newcastle upon Tyne
Tynemouth
South Shields
35–39
30–34
29
40–44
45–51
A6079
A69
Hexham
Corbridge
R Tyne
Wylam
Gateshead
A695
A19
A68
Consett
Washington
Sunderland
North Pennines
Chester-le-Street
A691
A690
Seaham
A182
Wearhead
Durham
A181
Peterlee

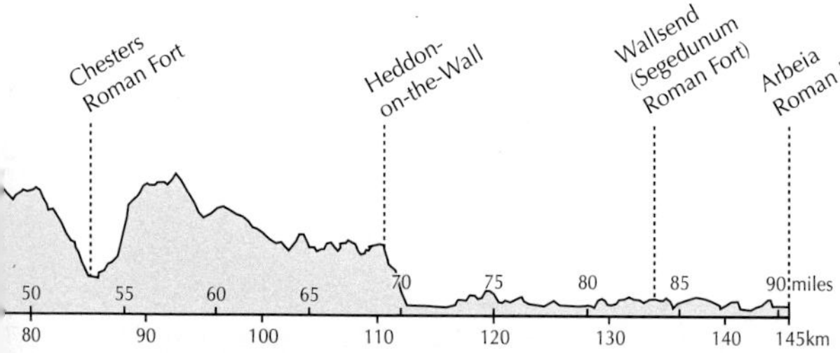

Chesters Roman Fort
Heddon-on-the-Wall
Wallsend (Segedunum Roman Fort)
Arbeia Roman Fort
50 55 60 65 70 75 80 85 90 miles
80 90 100 110 120 130 140 145km

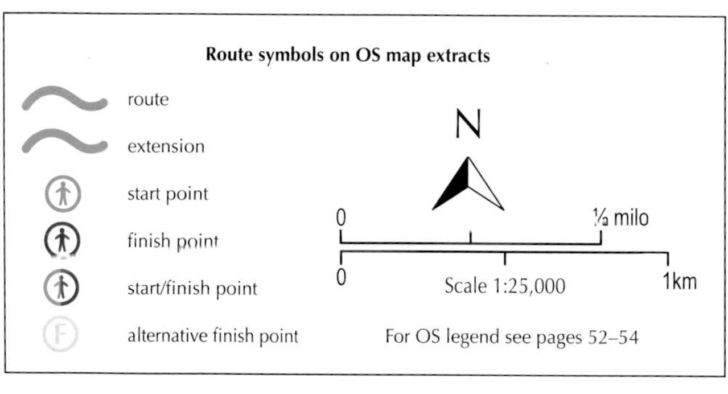

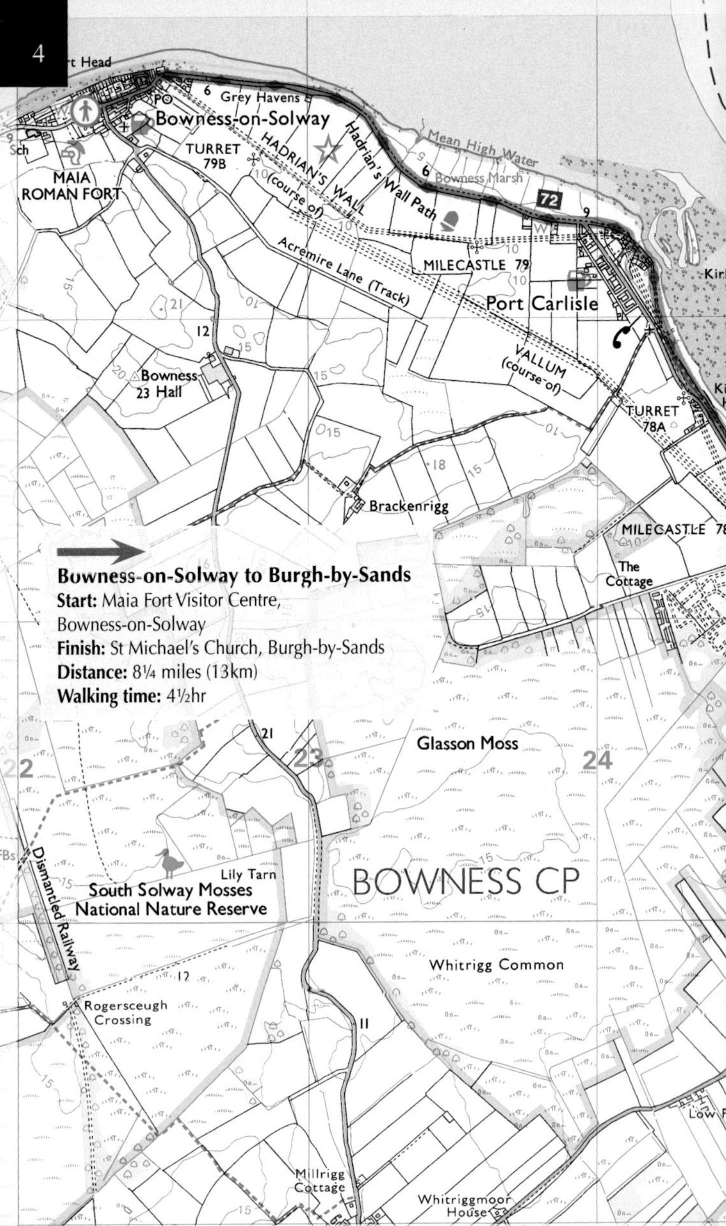

Bowness-on-Solway to Burgh-by-Sands

Start: Maia Fort Visitor Centre, Bowness-on-Solway

Finish: St Michael's Church, Burgh-by-Sands

Distance: 8¼ miles (13km)

Walking time: 4½hr

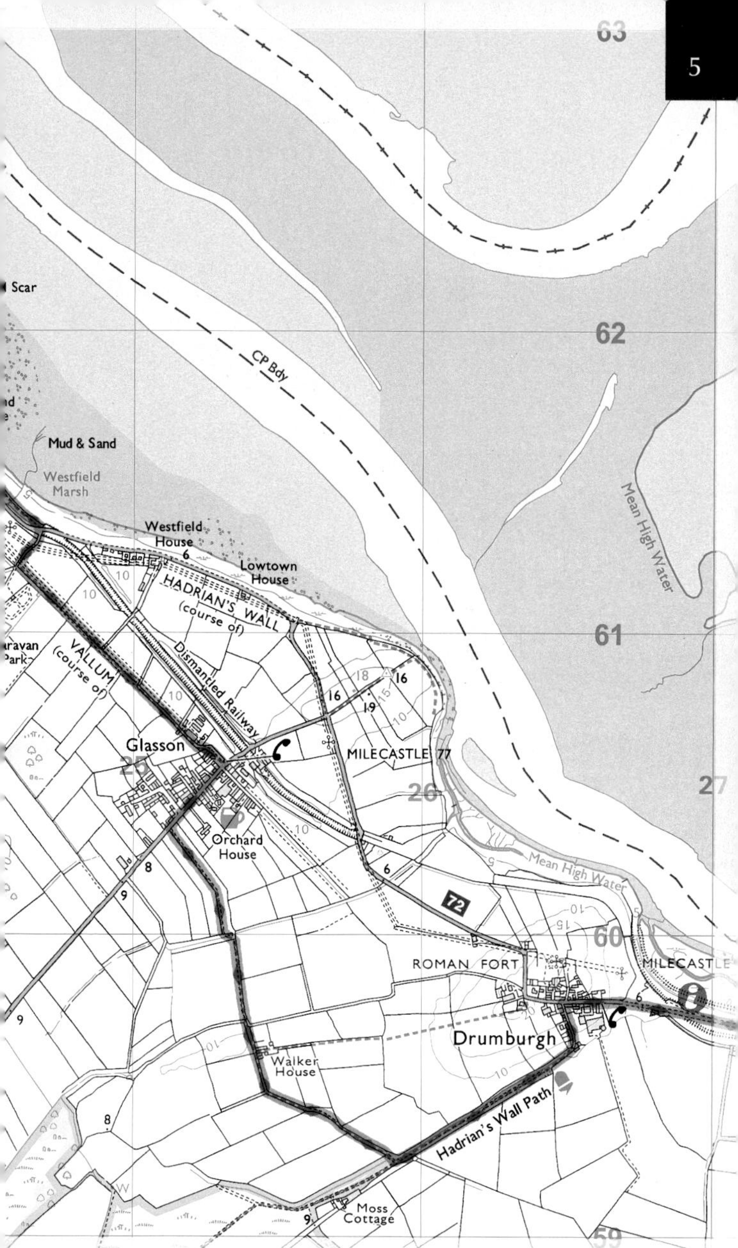
63
62
61
60
Scar
CP Bdy
Mud & Sand
Westfield Marsh
Westfield House
Lowtown House
HADRIAN'S WALL (course of)
VALLUM (course of)
Dismantled Railway
Glasson
MILECASTLE 77
Orchard House
Mean High Water
Mean High Water
72
ROMAN FORT
MILECASTLE
Drumburgh
Walker House
Hadrian's Wall Path
Moss Cottage
25
26
27

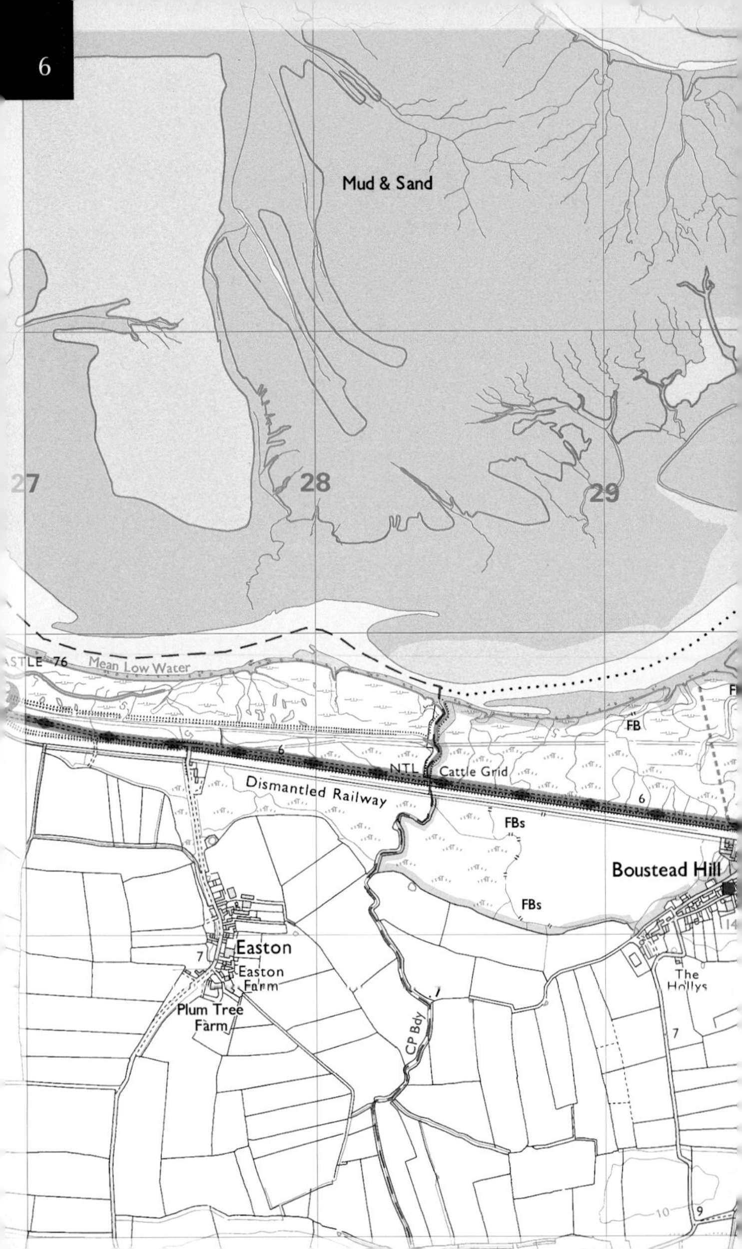

Mud & Sand
27
28
29
ASTLE 76
Mean Low Water
FB
6
NTL
Cattle Grid
Dismantled Railway
6
FBs
Boustead Hill
FBs
14
Easton
7
Easton
Farm
Plum Tree
Farm
The
Hollys
CP Bdy
7
10
9

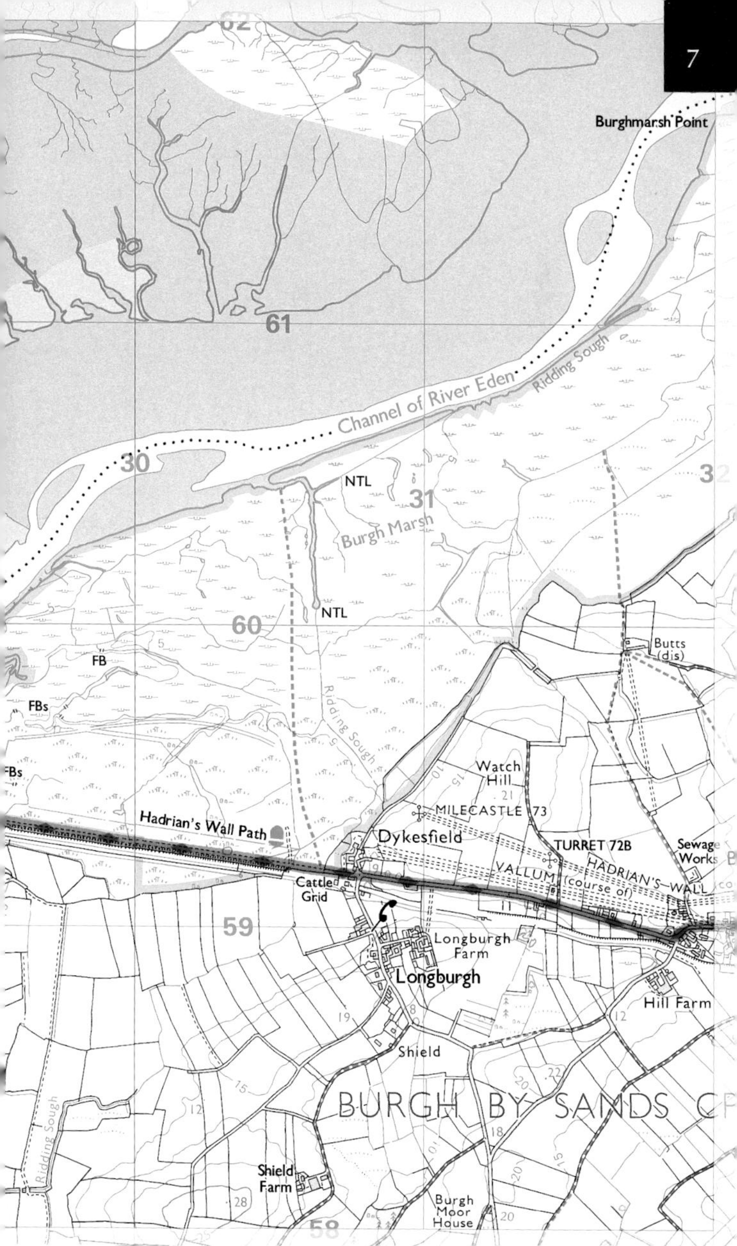

Burghmarsh Point
Channel of River Eden
Ridding Sough
NTL
Burgh Marsh
NTL
FB
FBs
FBs
Butts (dis)
Ridding Sough
Watch Hill
MILECASTLE 73
Hadrian's Wall Path
Dykesfield
TURRET 72B
Sewage Works
HADRIAN'S WALL
VALLUM (course of)
Cattle Grid
Longburgh Farm
Longburgh
Hill Farm
Shield
BURGH BY SANDS
Ridding Sough
Shield Farm
Burgh Moor House

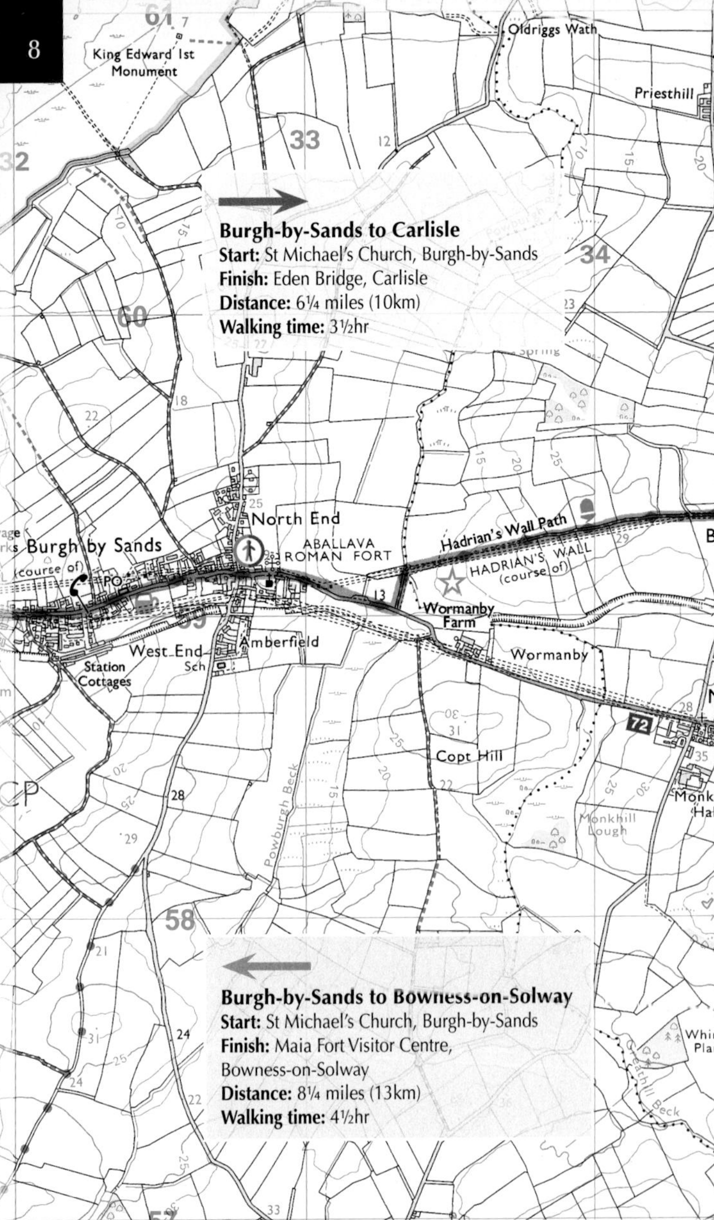

Burgh-by-Sands to Carlisle
Start: St Michael's Church, Burgh-by-Sands
Finish: Eden Bridge, Carlisle
Distance: 6¼ miles (10km)
Walking time: 3½hr

Burgh-by-Sands to Bowness-on-Solway
Start: St Michael's Church, Burgh-by-Sands
Finish: Maia Fort Visitor Centre, Bowness-on-Solway
Distance: 8¼ miles (13km)
Walking time: 4½hr

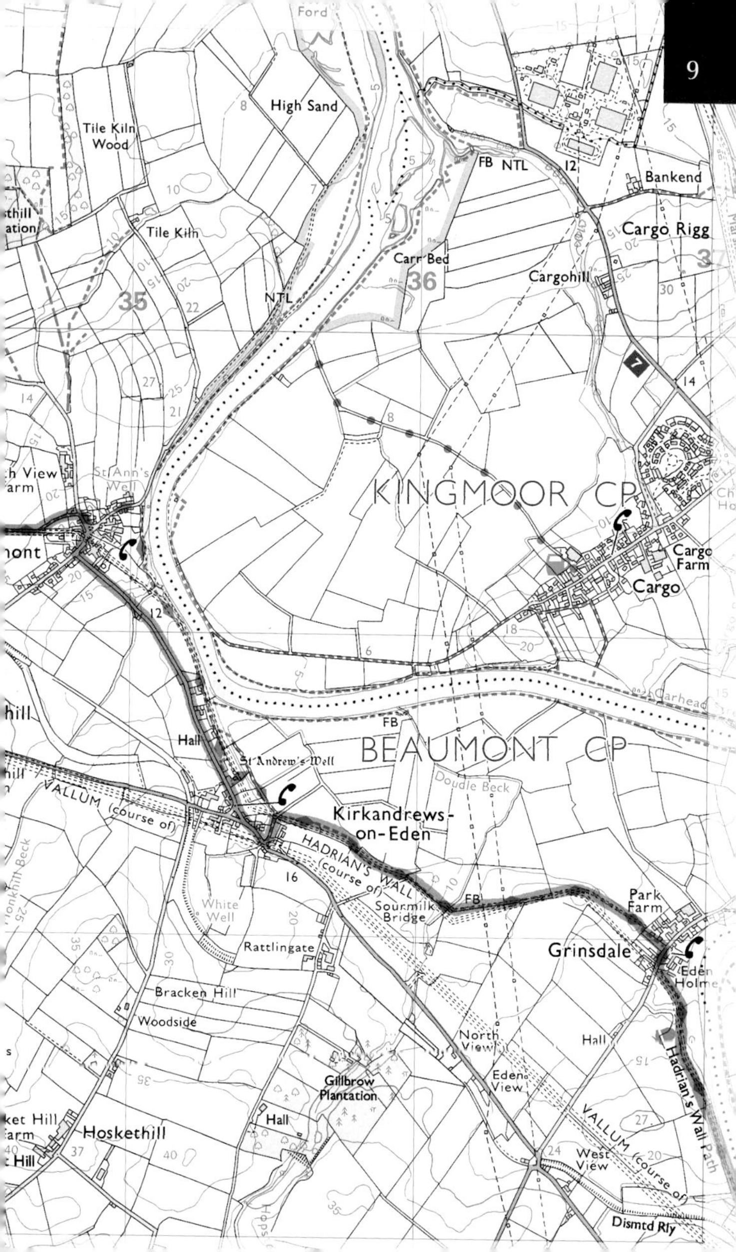
Ford
High Sand
Tile Kiln Wood
Tile Kiln
FB
NTL
Bankend
Cargo Rigg
Carr Bed
Cargohill
NTL
St Ann's Well
KINGMOOR CP
Cargo Farm
Cargo
Carhead
FB
Hall
BEAUMONT CP
St Andrew's Well
Doudle Beck
VALLUM (course of)
Kirkandrews-on-Eden
HADRIAN'S WALL (course of)
FB
Sourmilk Bridge
Park Farm
White Well
Rattlingate
Grinsdale
Eden Holme
Bracken Hill
Woodside
North View
Hall
Eden View
Gillbrow Plantation
Hadrian's Wall Path
Hall
Hoskethill
VALLUM (course of)
West View
Dismtd Rly

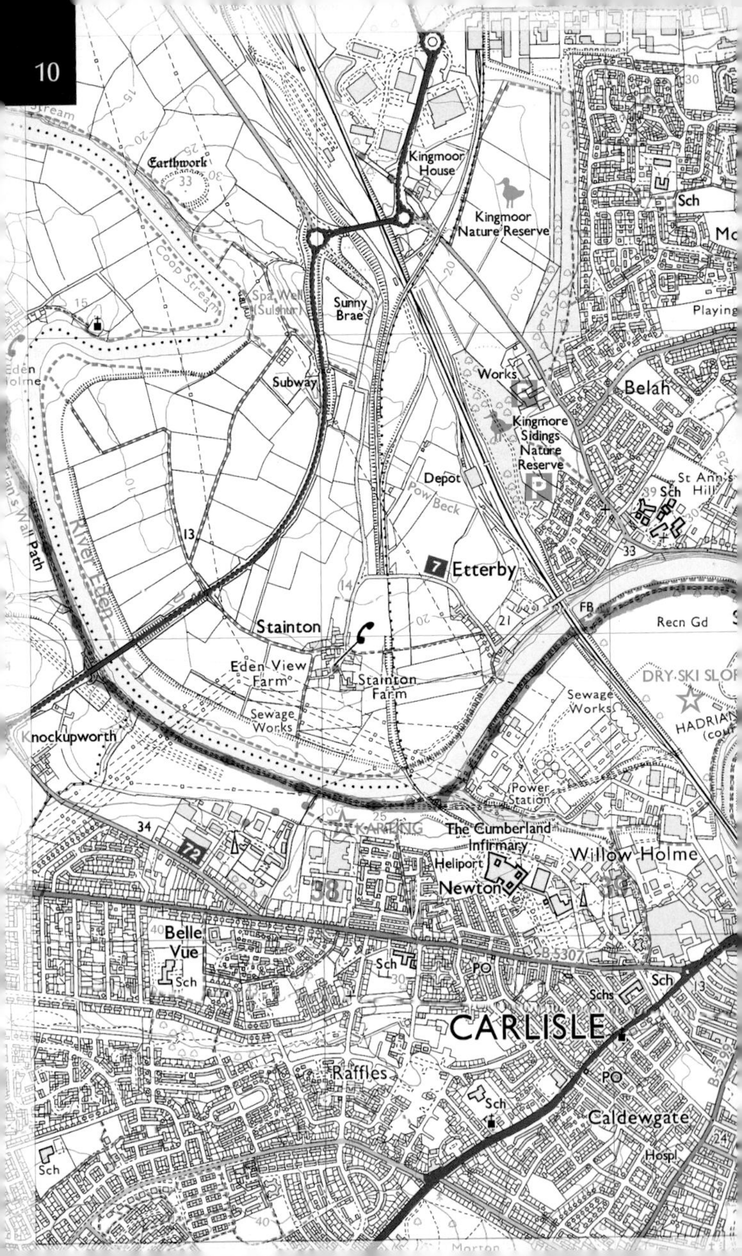

Stream
Earthwork
Coop Stream
Spa Well (Sulshur)
Kingmoor House
Kingmoor Nature Reserve
Sch
Sunny Brae
Playing
Eden Holme
Subway
Works
Belah
Kingmore Sidings Nature Reserve
Depot
Pow Beck
St Ann's Hill
Sch
River Eden
Hadrian's Wall Path
Etterby
Stainton
FB
Recn Gd
Eden View Farm
Stainton Farm
DRY SKI SLOPE
Sewage Works
Sewage Works
Knockupworth
Power Station
KARTING
The Cumberland Infirmary
Heliport
Willow Holme
Newton
Belle Vue
Sch
Sch
B 5307
PO
Sch
Schs
CARLISLE
Raffles
PO
Sch
Caldewgate
Hospl
Sch
Morton

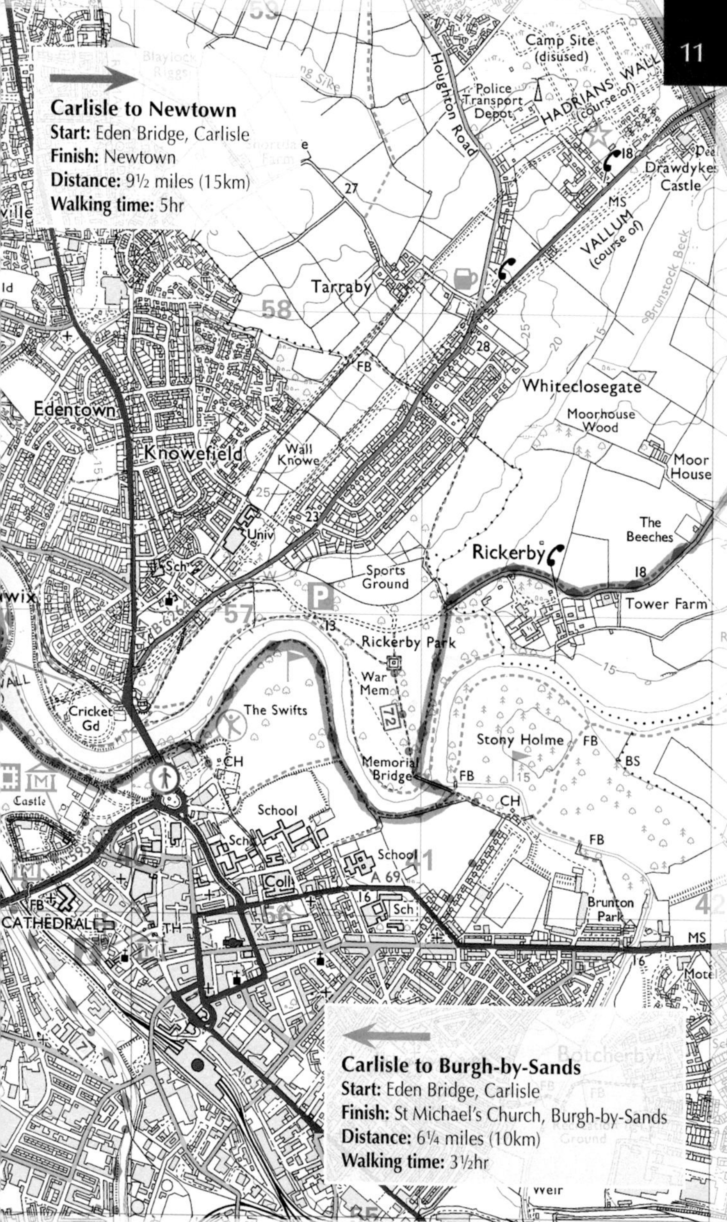

Carlisle to Newtown

Start: Eden Bridge, Carlisle
Finish: Newtown
Distance: 9½ miles (15km)
Walking time: 5hr

Carlisle to Burgh-by-Sands

Start: Eden Bridge, Carlisle
Finish: St Michael's Church, Burgh-by-Sands
Distance: 6¼ miles (10km)
Walking time: 3½hr

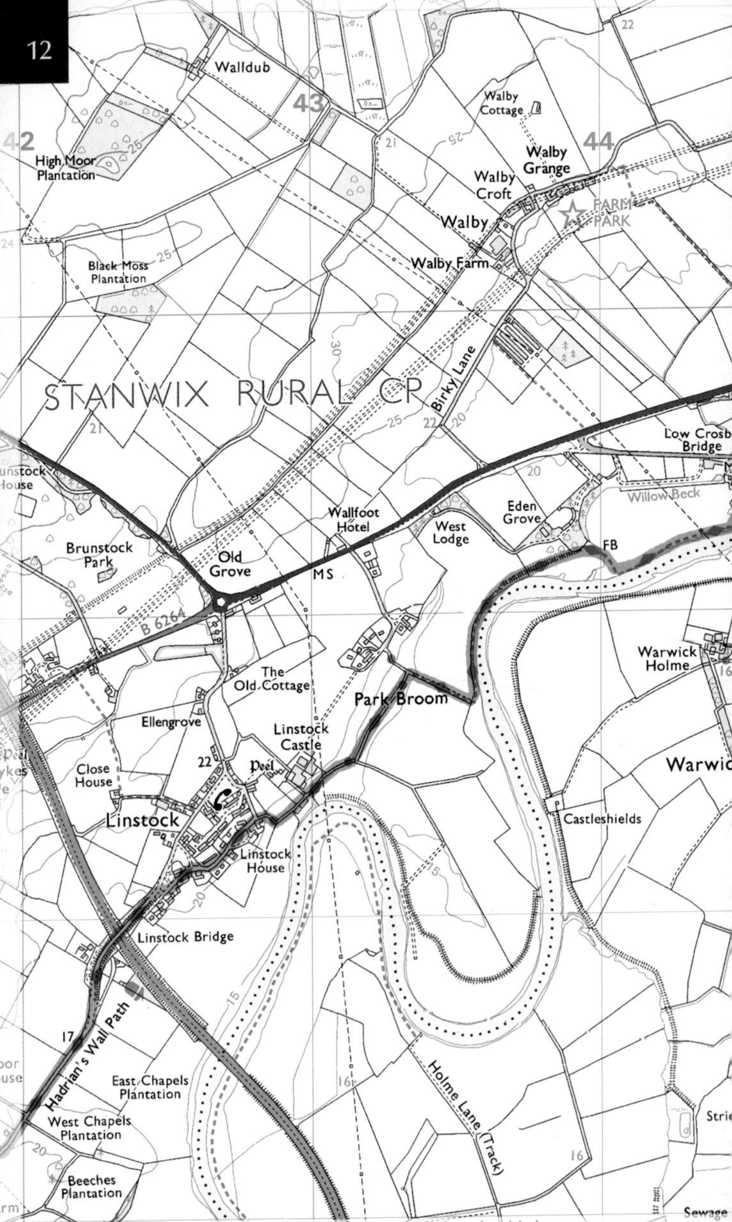

Walldub
43
42
High Moor Plantation
Walby Cottage
44
Walby Grange
Walby Croft
FARM PARK
Walby
Walby Farm
Black Moss Plantation
Birky Lane
STANWIX RURAL CP
Low Crosby Bridge
Willow Beck
Eden Grove
West Lodge
Wallfoot Hotel
FB
Brunstock Park
Old Grove
MS
B 6264
Warwick Holme
The Old Cottage
Park Broom
Ellengrove
Linstock Castle
Warwic
Close House
Peel
Linstock
Castleshields
Linstock House
Linstock Bridge
Hadrian's Wall Path
Holme Lane (Track)
East Chapels Plantation
West Chapels Plantation
Beeches Plantation
Scotby Holmes
Sewage Works

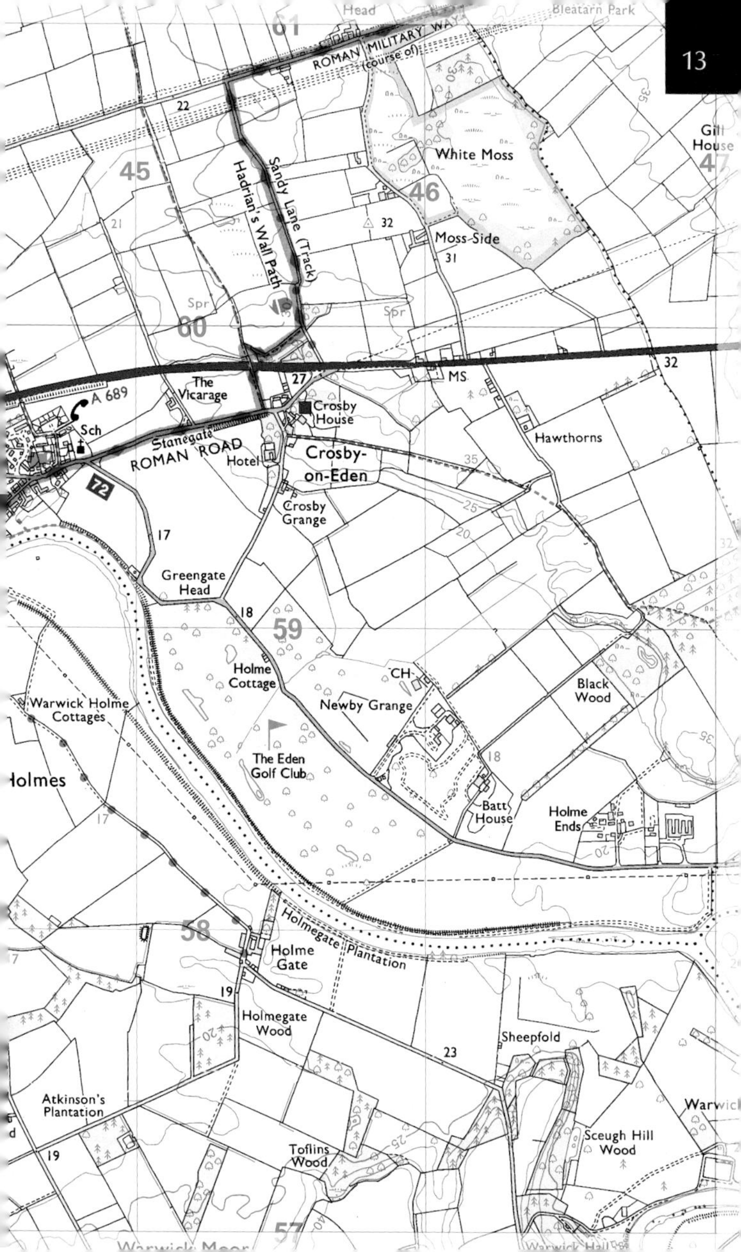
Head
Bleatarn Park
ROMAN MILITARY WAY
(course of)
White Moss
Gill House
Moss Side
Sandy Lane (Track)
Hadrian's Wall Path
Spr
Spr
A 689
The Vicarage
Sch
Stanegate
ROMAN ROAD
Hotel
Crosby House
Crosby-on-Eden
MS
Hawthorns
72
Crosby Grange
Greengate Head
Holme Cottage
CH
Newby Grange
Black Wood
Warwick Holme Cottages
The Eden Golf Club
Batt House
Holme Ends
Holmes
Holmegate Plantation
Holme Gate
Holmegate Wood
Sheepfold
Atkinson's Plantation
Toflins Wood
Sceugh Hill Wood

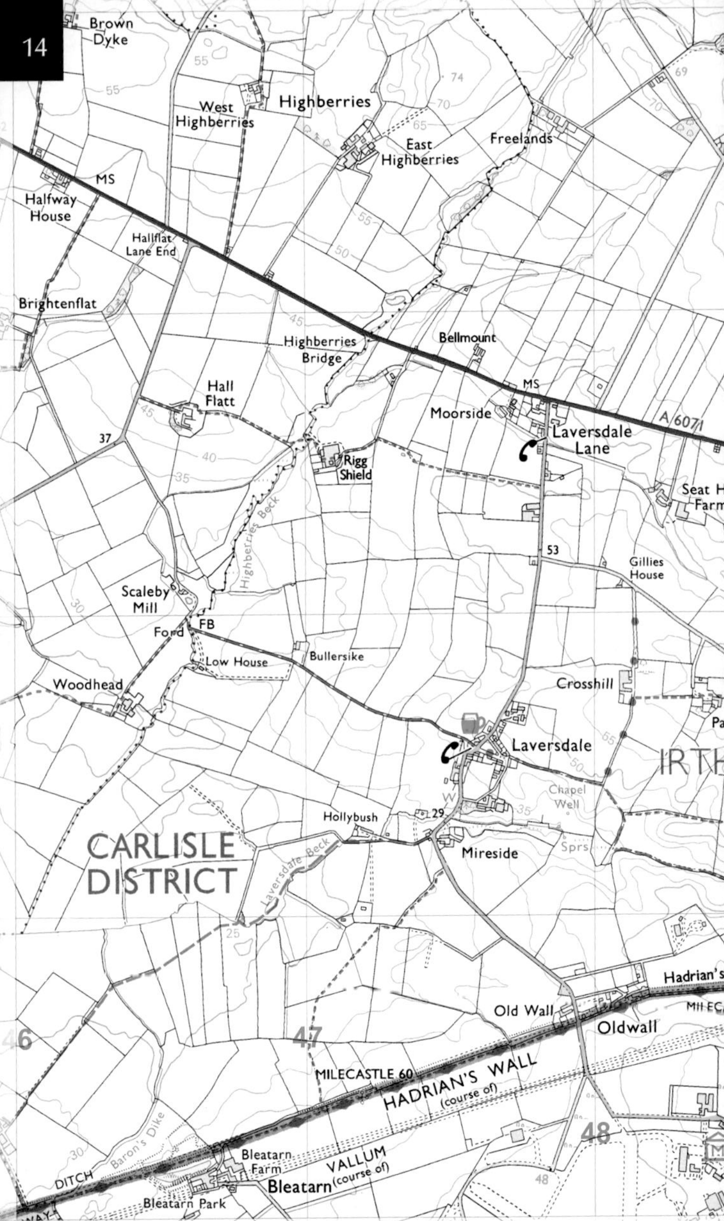
Brown Dyke
Highberries
West Highberries
East Highberries
Freelands
Halfway House
MS
Hallflat Lane End
Brightenflat
Highberries Bridge
Bellmount
Hall Flatt
Moorside
Laversdale Lane
A 6071
Rigg Shield
Seat H
Farm
53
Gillies House
Highberries Beck
Scaleby Mill
Ford
FB
Low House
Bullersike
Woodhead
Crosshill
Laversdale
IRTH
Chapel Well
Hollybush
29
Mireside
Sprs
CARLISLE DISTRICT
Laversdale Beck
Hadrian's
Old Wall
Oldwall
MILECASTLE 60
HADRIAN'S WALL
(course of)
Baron's Dike
DITCH
Bleatarn Farm
Bleatarn
VALLUM
(course of)
Bleatarn Park
46
47
48
37

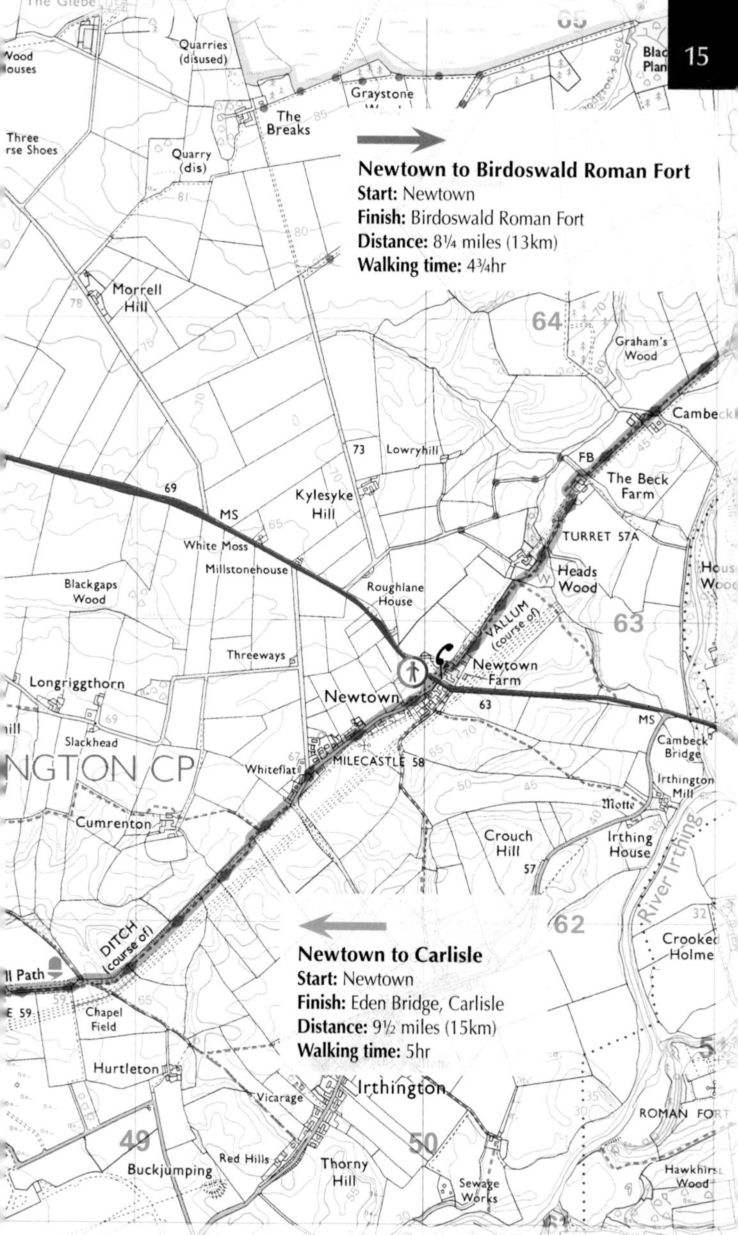

Newtown to Birdoswald Roman Fort
Start: Newtown
Finish: Birdoswald Roman Fort
Distance: 8¼ miles (13km)
Walking time: 4¾hr

Newtown to Carlisle
Start: Newtown
Finish: Eden Bridge, Carlisle
Distance: 9½ miles (15km)
Walking time: 5hr

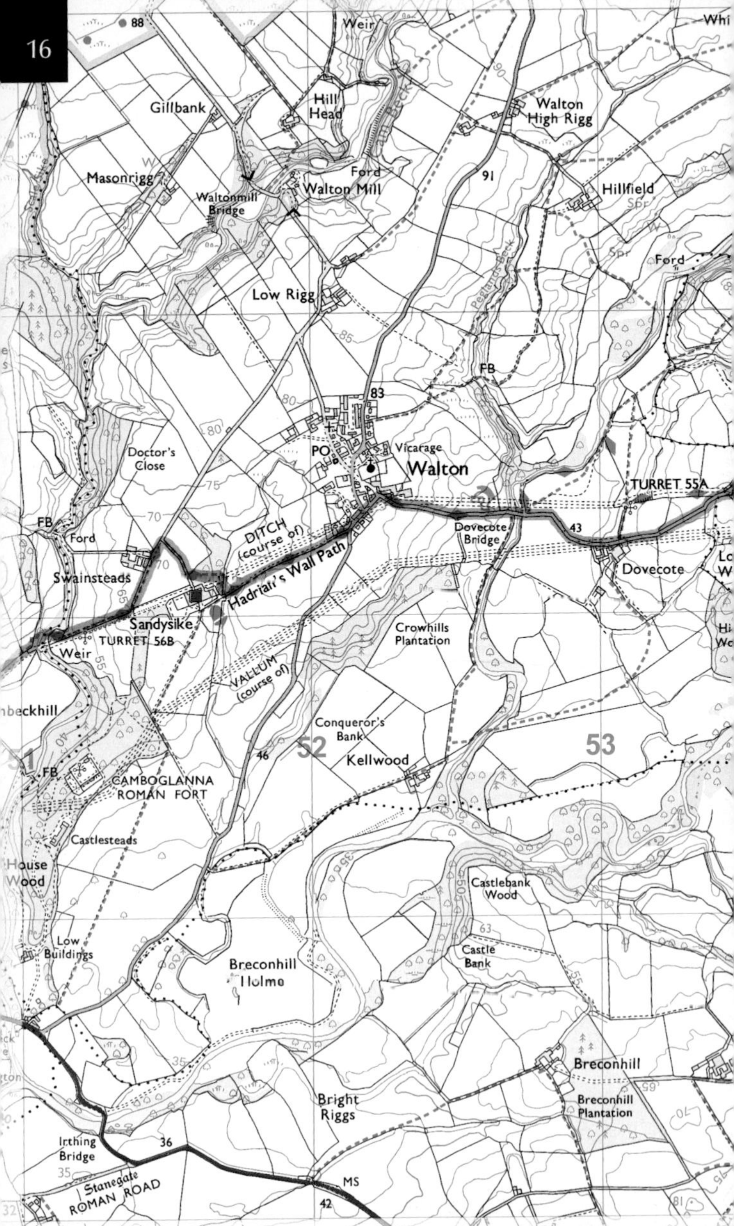
Weir
Gillbank
Hill Head
Walton High Rigg
Masonrigg
Ford
Walton Mill
Waltonmill Bridge
Hillfield
Low Rigg
Ford
Pegglands Beck
FB
83
Doctor's Close
PO
Vicarage
Walton
TURRET 55A
FB
Ford
Swainsteads
DITCH (course of)
Hadrian's Wall Path
Dovecote Bridge
43
Dovecote
Sandysike
TURRET 56B
Weir
Crowhills Plantation
VALLUM (course of)
Conqueror's Bank
52
53
Kellwood
46
FB
CAMBOGLANNA ROMAN FORT
Castlesteads
House Wood
Castlebank Wood
Castle Bank
Low Buildings
Breconhill Holme
Breconhill
Breconhill Plantation
Bright Riggs
Irthing Bridge
36
Stanegate ROMAN ROAD
MS
42

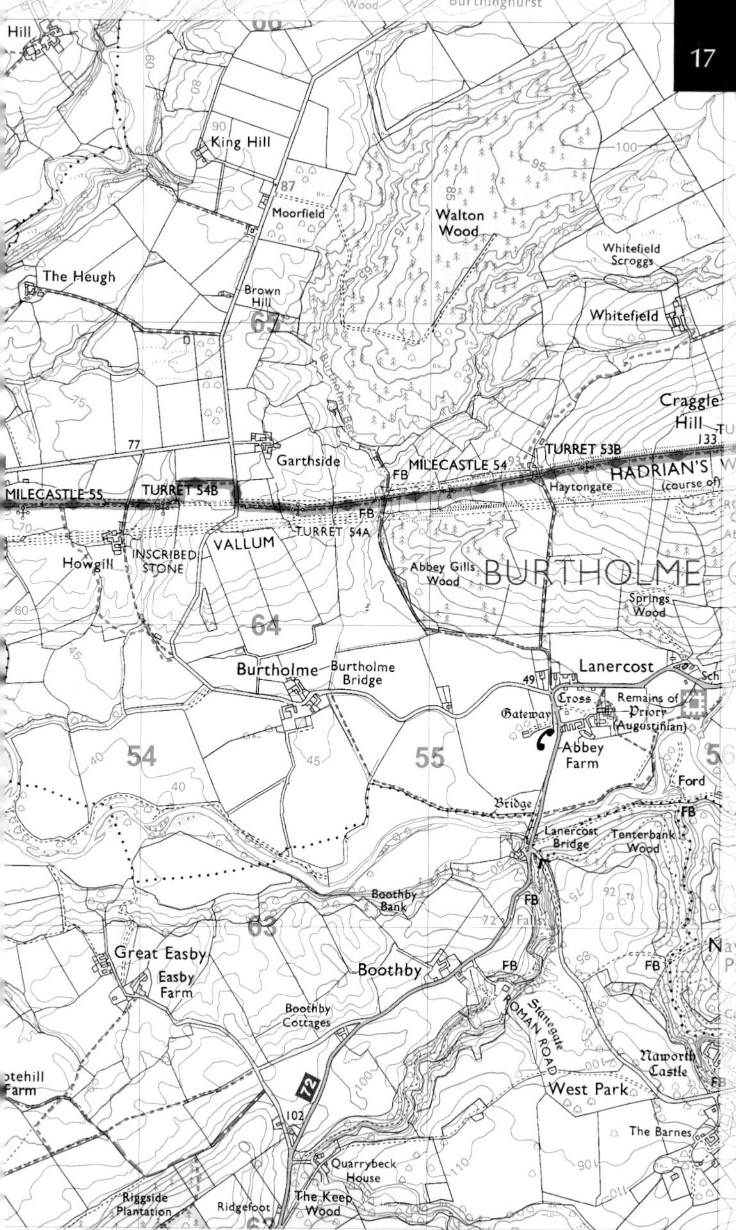

Burthinghurst
Wood
Hill
King Hill
Moorfield
Walton Wood
Whitefield Scroggs
Whitefield
The Heugh
Brown Hill
Craggle Hill
Garthside
TURRET 53B
MILECASTLE 54
HADRIAN'S
(course of)
Haytongate
MILECASTLE 55
TURRET 54B
TURRET 54A
FB
VALLUM
Howgill
INSCRIBED STONE
Abbey Gills Wood
BURTHOLME
Springs Wood
Burtholme
Burtholme Bridge
Lanercost
Sch
Cross
Gateway
Remains of Priory (Augustinian)
Abbey Farm
Ford
Bridge
Lanercost Bridge
Tenterbank Wood
Boothby Bank
Falls
Great Easby
Easby Farm
Boothby
Boothby Cottages
Stanegate
ROMAN ROAD
Naworth Castle
West Park
The Barnes
Quarrybeck House
The Keep Wood
Ridgefoot
Riggside Plantation
72
102

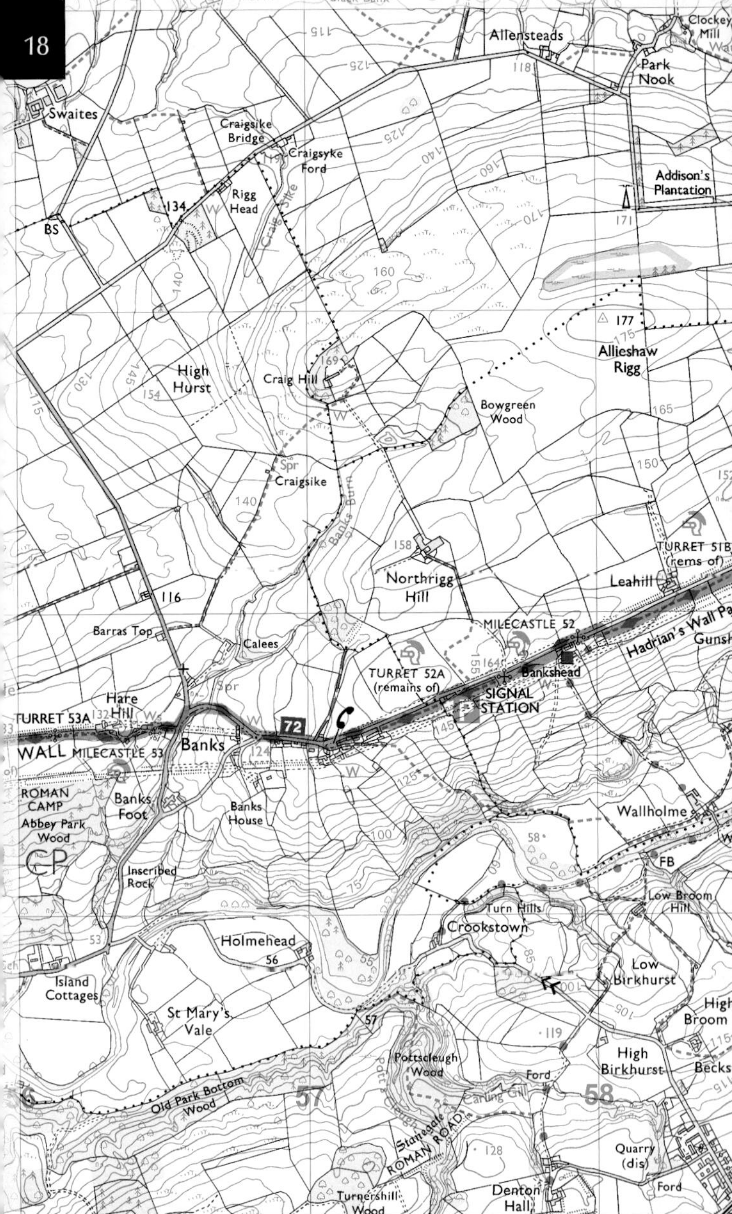
Farm
Black Bank
Allensteads
Clockey Mill
Park Nook
Swaites
Craigsike Bridge
Craigsyke Ford
Rigg Head
Craig Sike
Addison's Plantation
BS
Allieshaw Rigg
High Hurst
Craig Hill
Bowgreen Wood
Craigsike
Banks Burn
Northrigg Hill
TURRET 51B (rems of)
Leahill
Barras Top
Calees
MILECASTLE 52
Hadrian's Wall Pa
TURRET 52A (remains of)
Bankshead
SIGNAL STATION
Hare Hill
TURRET 53A
Banks
WALL
MILECASTLE 53
ROMAN CAMP
Banks Foot
Banks House
Abbey Park Wood
Wallholme
FB
Inscribed Rock
Low Broom Hill
Turn Hills
Crookstown
Holmehead
Island Cottages
Low Birkhurst
High Broom
St Mary's Vale
High Birkhurst
Becks
Pottscleugh Wood
Ford
Carling Gill
Old Park Bottom Wood
Stanegate ROMAN ROAD
Quarry (dis)
Turnershill Wood
Denton Hall
Ford

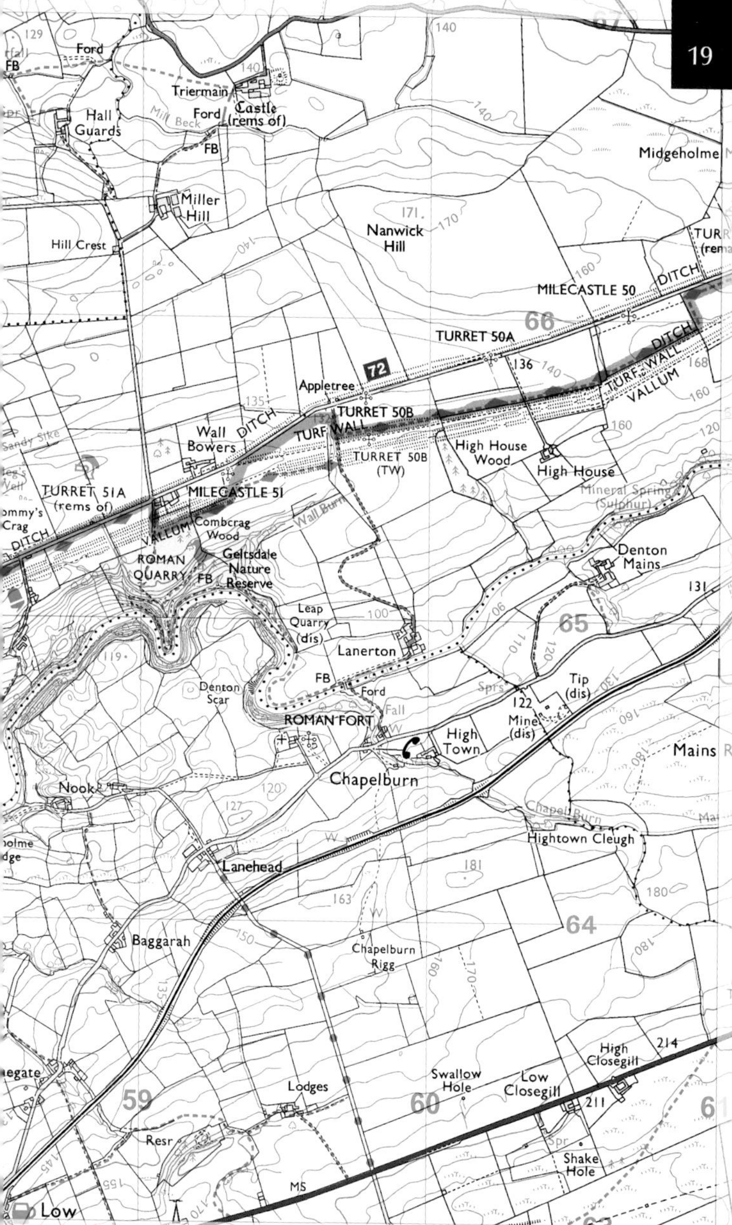
Ford
Triermain
Castle (rems of)
Ford
Hall Guards
Mill Beck
FB
Miller Hill
Hill Crest
Midgeholme
Nanwick Hill
MILECASTLE 50
TURRET 50A
DITCH
Appletree
TURRET 50B
TURF WALL
VALLUM
Wall Bowers
TURRET 50B (TW)
High House Wood
High House
TURRET 51A (rems of)
MILECASTLE 51
Combcrag Wood
Wall Burn
Mineral Spring (Sulphur)
ROMAN QUARRY
FB
Geltsdale Nature Reserve
Denton Mains
Leap Quarry (dis)
Lanerton
Denton Scar
FB
Ford
Fall
Tip (dis)
Mine (dis)
ROMAN FORT
High Town
Chapelburn
Mains
Nook
Chapel Burn
Hightown Cleugh
Lanehead
Baggarah
Chapelburn Rigg
High Closegill
Swallow Hole
Low Closegill
Lodges
Resr
Shake Hole
MS
Low

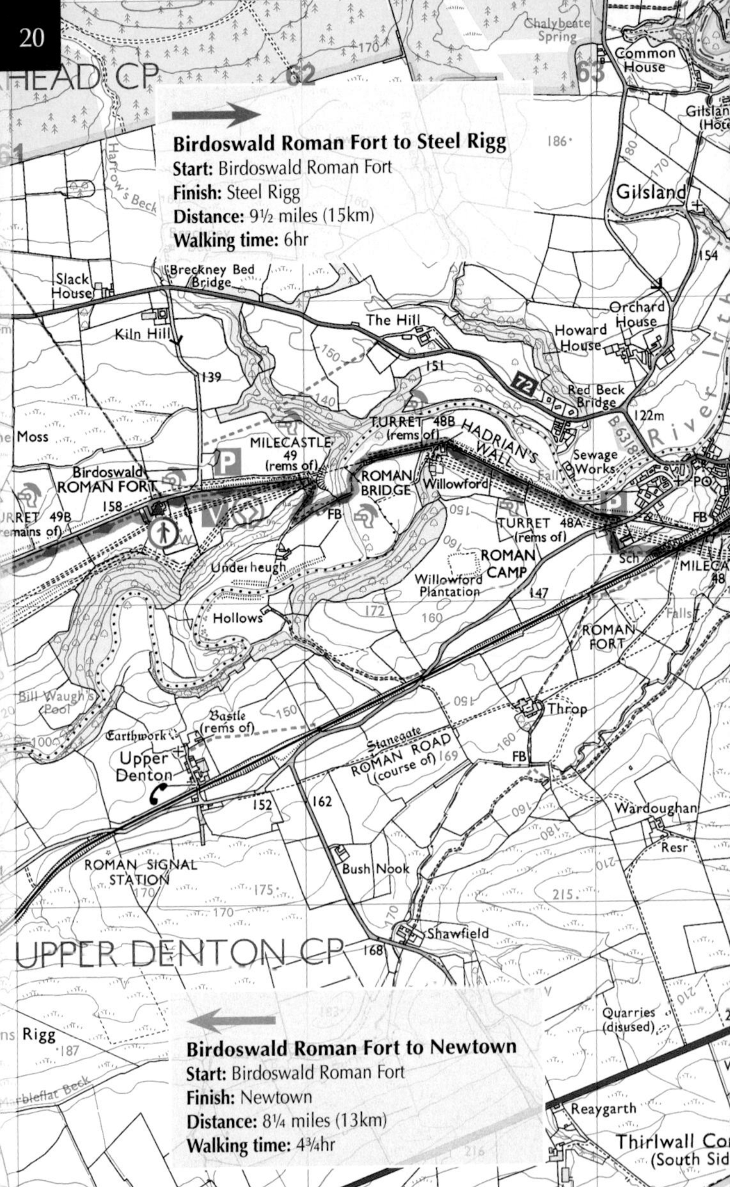
Birdoswald Roman Fort to Steel Rigg
Start: Birdoswald Roman Fort
Finish: Steel Rigg
Distance: 9½ miles (15km)
Walking time: 6hr
Birdoswald Roman Fort to Newtown
Start: Birdoswald Roman Fort
Finish: Newtown
Distance: 8¼ miles (13km)
Walking time: 4¾hr
The Height
Chalybeate Spring
Common House
Gilsland
Slack House
Breckney Bed Bridge
Kiln Hill
The Hill
Orchard House
Howard House
Red Beck Bridge
Moss
MILECASTLE 49 (rems of)
TURRET 48B (rems of)
HADRIAN'S WALL
Sewage Works
Birdoswald ROMAN FORT
ROMAN BRIDGE
Willowford
TURRET 49B (remains of)
TURRET 48A (rems of)
ROMAN CAMP
Underheugh
Willowford Plantation
Hollows
ROMAN FORT
Bill Waugh's Pool
Throp
Bastle (rems of)
Earthwork
Upper Denton
Stanegate ROMAN ROAD (course of)
Wardoughan
Resr
ROMAN SIGNAL STATION
Bush Nook
Shawfield
UPPER DENTON CP
Rigg
Quarries (disused)
Reaygarth
Thirlwall Co
(South Sid

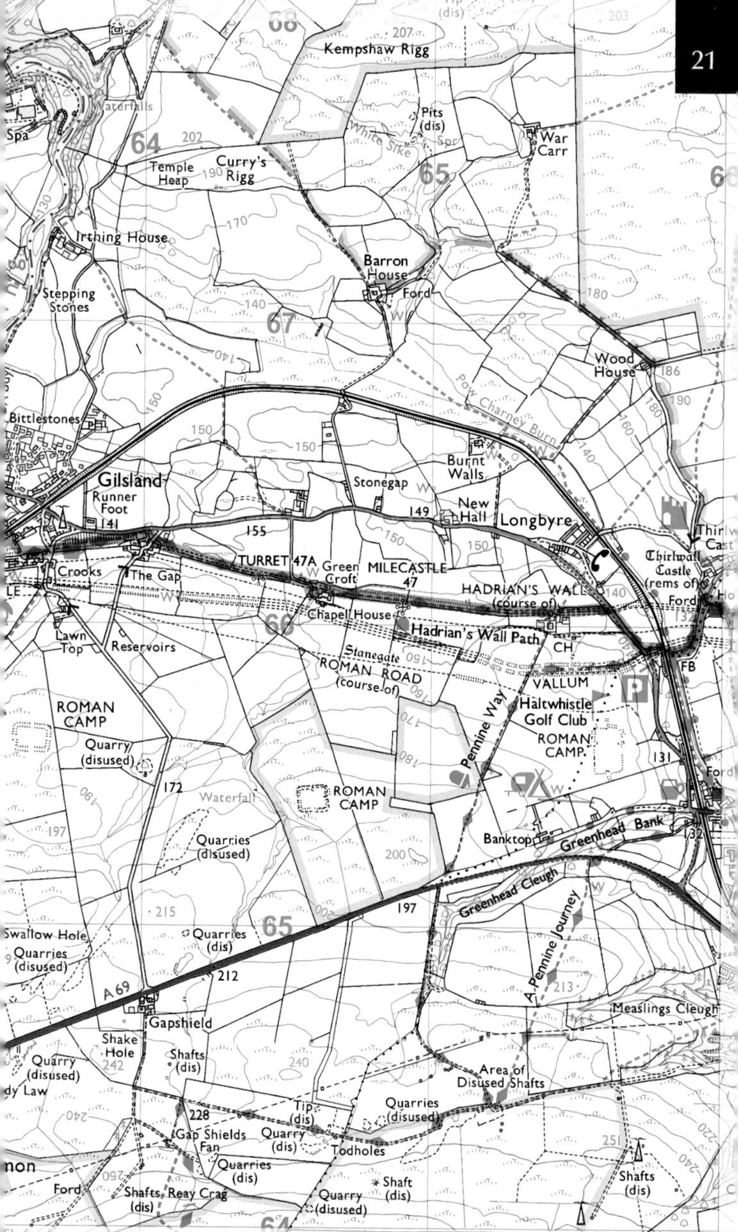
Kempshaw Rigg
Pits (dis)
War Carr
White Sike
Waterfalls
Spa
Temple Heap
Curry's Rigg
Irthing House
Barron House
Ford
Stepping Stones
Wood House
Pow Charney Burn
Bittlestones
Gilsland
Runner Foot
Stonegap
Burnt Walls
New Hall
Longbyre
Thirlwall Castle (rems of)
Crooks
The Gap
TURRET 47A
Green Croft
MILECASTLE 47
HADRIAN'S WALL (course of)
Chapel House
Hadrian's Wall Path
CH
FB
Lawn Top
Reservoirs
Stanegate ROMAN ROAD (course of)
VALLUM
Haltwhistle Golf Club
ROMAN CAMP
Pennine Way
ROMAN CAMP
Quarry (disused)
Waterfall
ROMAN CAMP
Banktop
Greenhead Bank
Quarries (disused)
Greenhead Cleugh
A Pennine Journey
Swallow Hole
Quarries (disused)
Quarries (dis)
A 69
Gapshield
Measlings Cleugh
Shake Hole
Shafts (dis)
Quarry (disused)
Area of Disused Shafts
Quarries (disused)
Tip (dis)
Gap Shields Fan
Quarry (dis)
Todholes
Quarries (dis)
Ford
Shafts (dis)
Reay Crag
Quarry (disused)
Shaft (dis)
Shafts (dis)

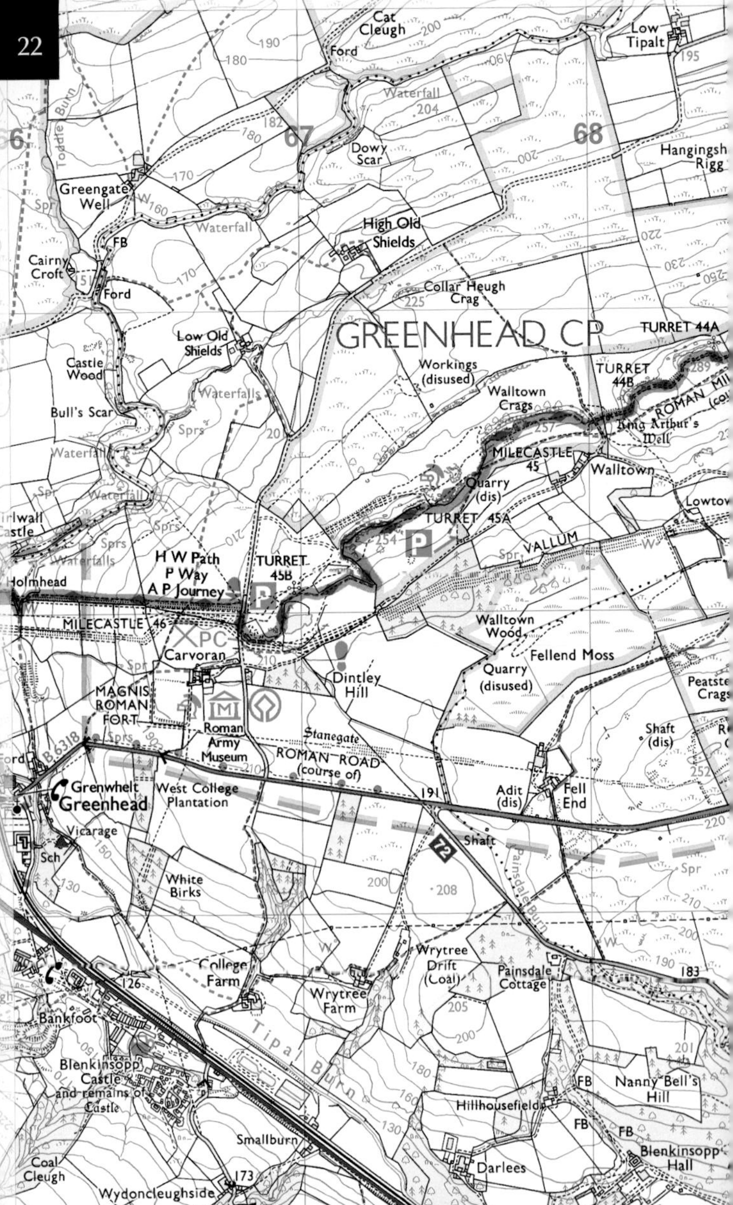
Cat Cleugh
Ford
Low Tipalt
Waterfall
Dowy Scar
Hangingshaw Rigg
Greengate Well
FB
Waterfall
High Old Shields
Cairny Croft
Ford
Collar Heugh Crag
GREENHEAD CP
TURRET 44A
Low Old Shields
Castle Wood
Workings (disused)
TURRET 44B
Walltown Crags
ROMAN MIL
King Arthur's Well
Bull's Scar
Waterfalls
MILECASTLE 45
Walltown
Quarry (dis)
TURRET 45A
VALLUM
Holmhead
H W Path
P Way
A P Journey
TURRET 45B
MILECASTLE 46
PC
Carvoran
Walltown Wood
Fellend Moss
Quarry (disused)
Dintley Hill
MAGNIS ROMAN FORT
Roman Army Museum
Stanegate
ROMAN ROAD (course of)
Shaft (dis)
Peatstey Crags
B 6318
Ford
Grenwhelt
Greenhead
West College Plantation
Adit (dis)
Fell End
Vicarage
Sch
Shaft
Painsdale Burn
White Birks
Wrytree Drift (Coal)
Painsdale Cottage
College Farm
Wrytree Farm
Bankfoot
Tipal Burn
Blenkinsopp Castle and remains of Castle
Nanny Bell's Hill
Hillhousefield
FB
Smallburn
Darlees
Blenkinsopp Hall
Coal Cleugh
Wydoncleughside

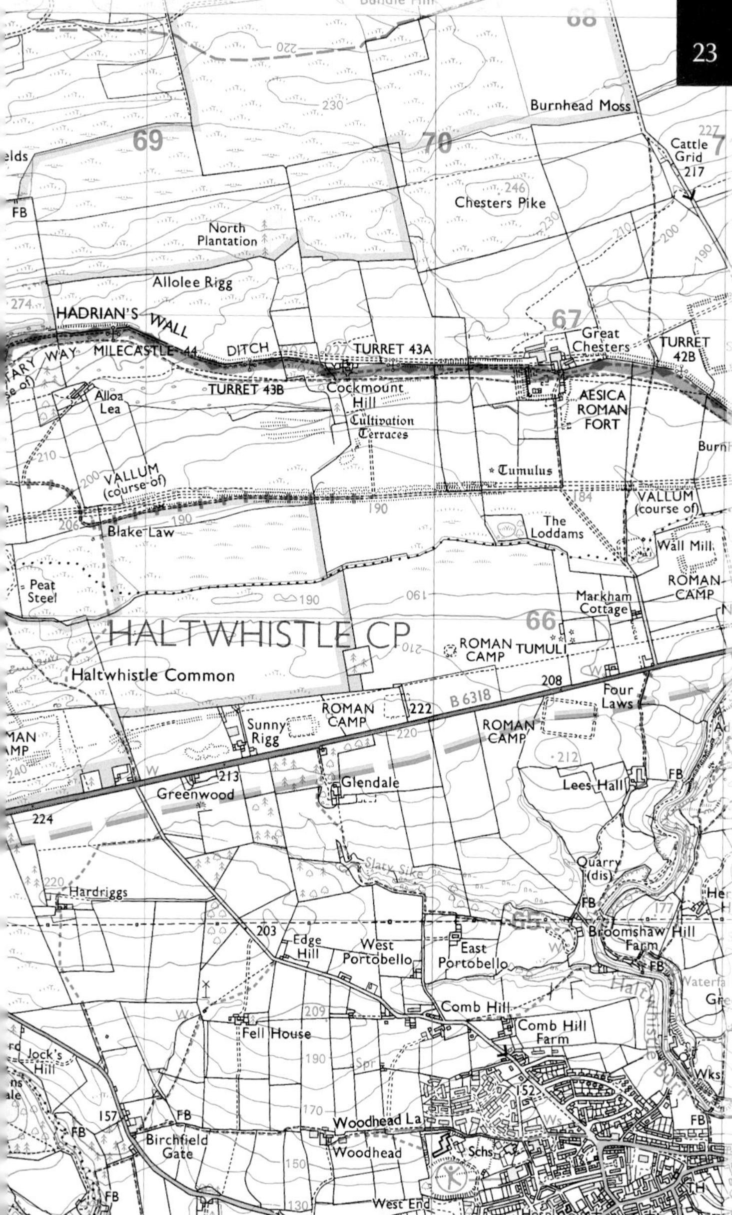
Bundle Hill
Burnhead Moss
Cattle Grid
Chesters Pike
North Plantation
Allolee Rigg
HADRIAN'S WALL
MILECASTLE 44
DITCH
TURRET 43A
TURRET 43B
Great Chesters
TURRET 42B
Alloa Lea
Cockmount Hill
Cultivation Terraces
AESICA ROMAN FORT
Tumulus
VALLUM (course of)
Blake Law
The Loddams
Wall Mill
ROMAN CAMP
Peat Steel
Markham Cottage
HALTWHISTLE CP
ROMAN CAMP
TUMULI
Haltwhistle Common
Four Laws
Sunny Rigg
B 6318
Greenwood
Glendale
Lees Hall
Quarry (dis)
Slaty Sike
Hardriggs
Broomshaw Hill Farm
Edge Hill
West Portobello
East Portobello
Haltwhistle Burn
Comb Hill
Fell House
Comb Hill Farm
Jock's Hill
Woodhead La
Birchfield Gate
Woodhead
Schs
West End
Hosp

Wealside
High Edges Green
Edges Green
Brown Rigg
ROMAN AQUEDUCT (course of)
ROMAN AQUEDUCT (course of)
Pont Gallon Burn
Ventners Hall
Bullyhouse Rigg
Longsyke
Caw Burn
Cawburn Shield
H Ram
High Close a Burns
Close a Burns
Bridge End
Sook Hill
ROMAN AQUEDUCT (course of)
Low Close a Burns
Cleughfoot
Melkridge C
Hexagon Plantation
FB
MELKRIDGE C
East Cawfields
P Way
H W Path
MILECASTLE 41
Cawfields
TURRET 41B
Thorny Doors
TURRET 41A
Caw Gap
Bogle Hole
ROMAN CAMPS
Hole Gap
Cawfield Crags
Thorny Doors
A Pennine Journey
ROMAN MILITARY WAY (course of)
MILECASTLE 42
Quarry (disused)
Resr
Shield on the Wall
Mare & Foal
PC
ROMAN CAMPS
Level (dis)
MS
Milestone House
Stanegate
ROMAN ROAD (course of)
ROMAN FORT
New Bridge
ROMAN CAMP
Moor Cottage
Hallpeat Moss
Hill Top
Melkridge Tilery
The Holme
Adit
Mineral Workings (disused)
The Doors Farm
Shield Hill
Dour Crags
Oaky Knowe Crags
Sheepfold
High Plantation
Moorfield House
Herding Hill
Comm

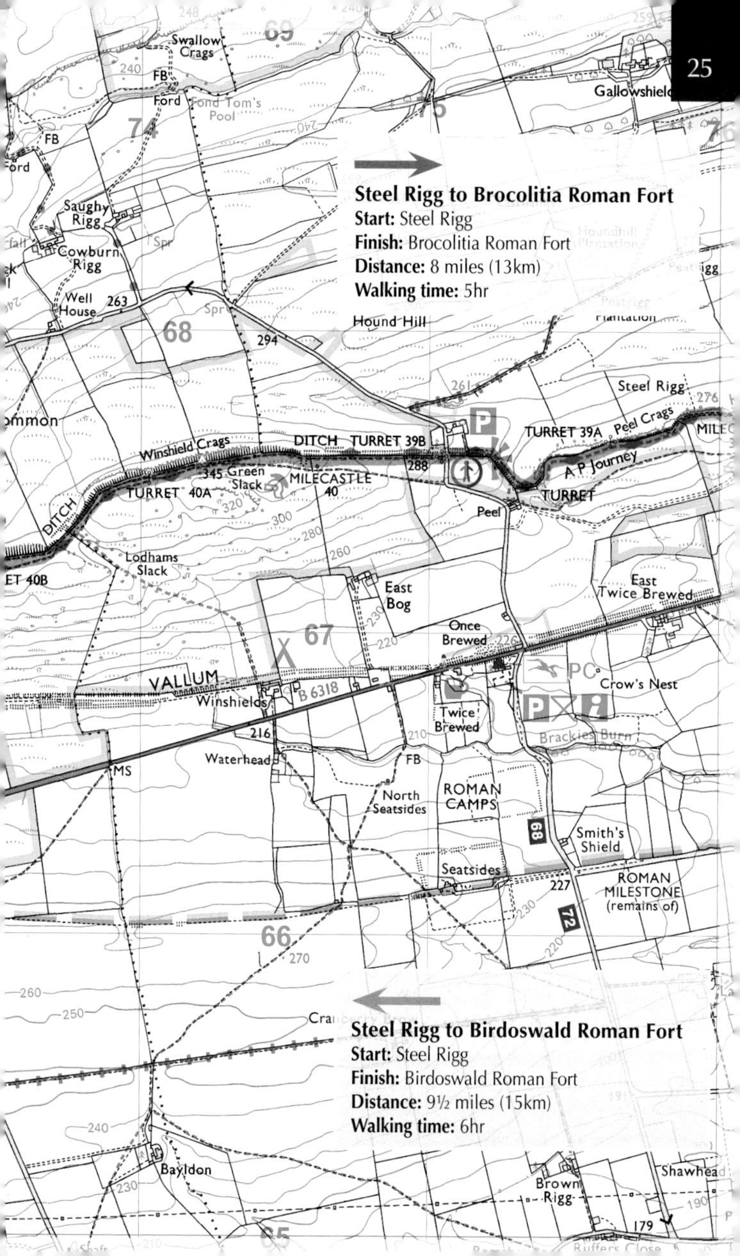

Steel Rigg to Brocolitia Roman Fort

Start: Steel Rigg
Finish: Brocolitia Roman Fort
Distance: 8 miles (13km)
Walking time: 5hr

Steel Rigg to Birdoswald Roman Fort

Start: Steel Rigg
Finish: Birdoswald Roman Fort
Distance: 9½ miles (15km)
Walking time: 6hr

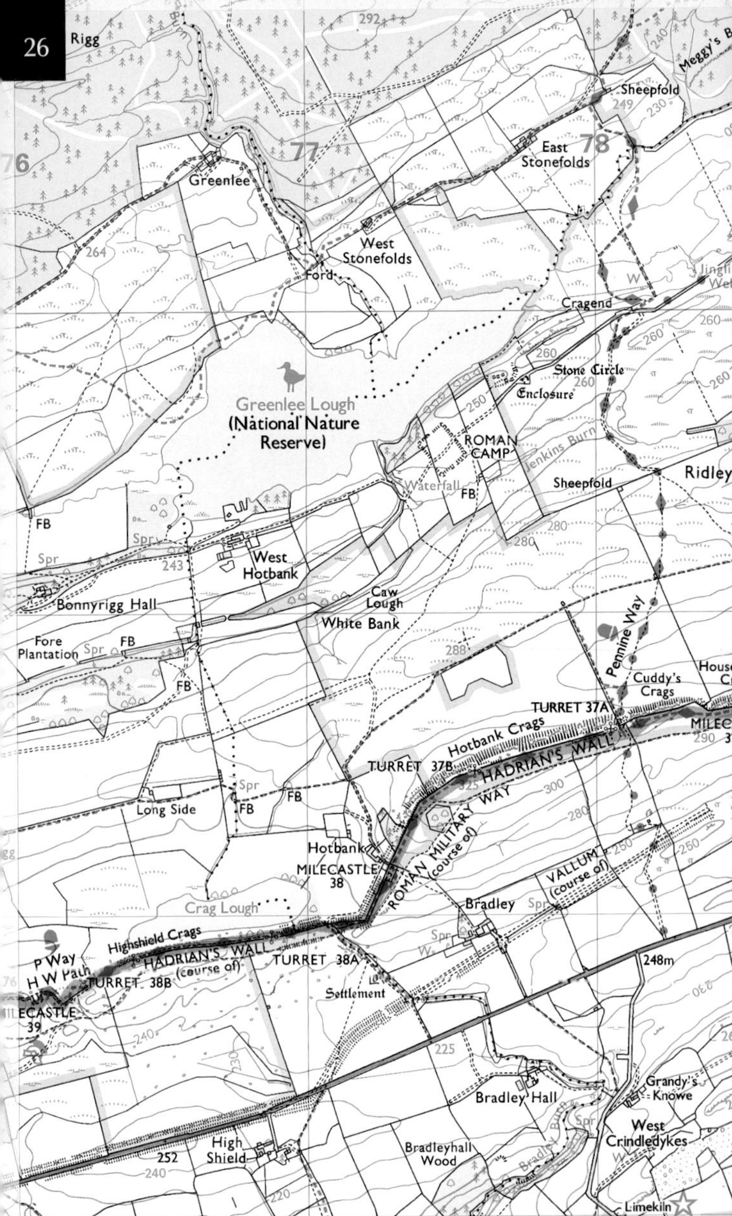
Rigg
Greenlee
West Stonefolds
East Stonefolds
Sheepfold
Ford
Cragend
Stone Circle
Enclosure
Greenlee Lough
(National Nature Reserve)
ROMAN CAMP
Jenkins Burn
Waterfall
Sheepfold
Ridley
West Hotbank
Bonnyrigg Hall
Caw Lough
White Bank
Fore Plantation
Pennine Way
Cuddy's Crags
TURRET 37A
Hotbank Crags
HADRIAN'S WALL
TURRET 37B
ROMAN MILITARY WAY (course of)
Long Side
Hotbank
MILECASTLE 38
VALLUM (course of)
Bradley
Crag Lough
Highshield Crags
HADRIAN'S WALL (course of)
TURRET 38A
TURRET 38B
P Way
H W Path
MILECASTLE 39
Settlement
Bradley Hall
Grandy's Knowe
West Crindledykes
High Shield
Bradleyhall Wood
Limekiln
Sheepfold
248m

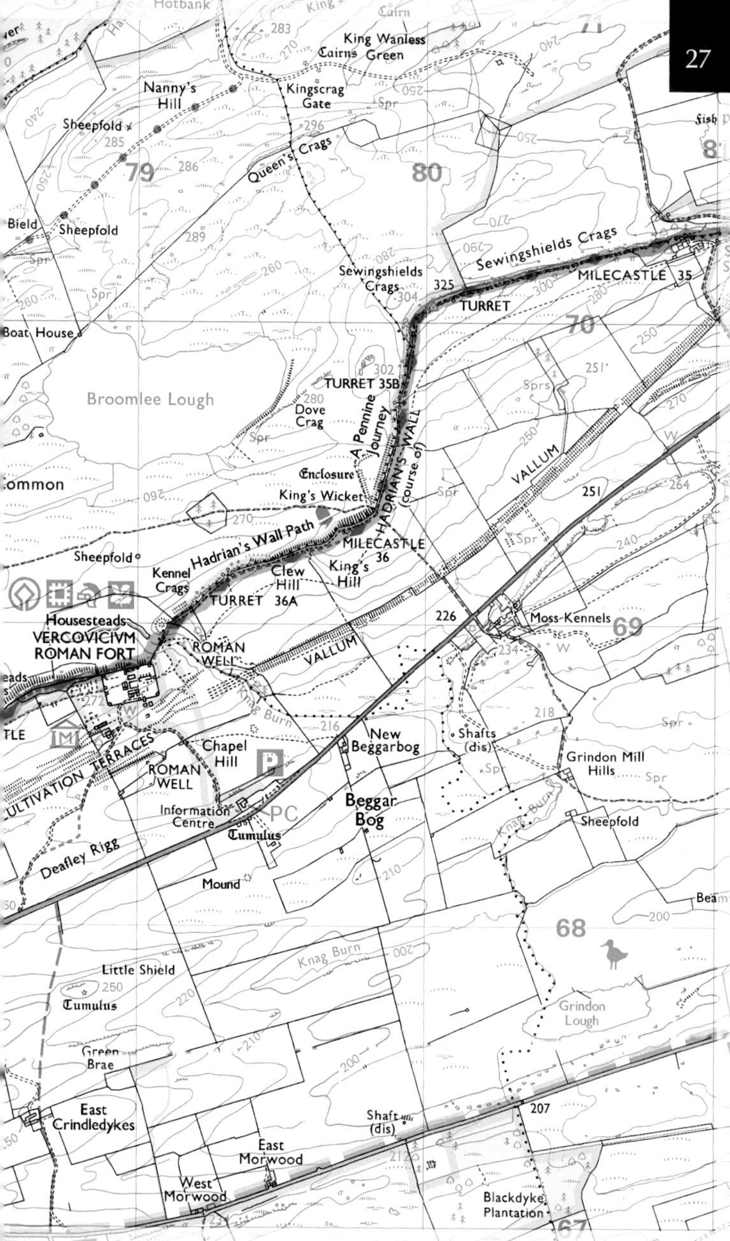
Hotbank
King Wanless Green
Cairns
Cairn
Nanny's Hill
Kingscrag Gate
Sheepfold
Queen's Crags
Bield
Sheepfold
Sewingshields Crags
Sewingshields Crags
MILECASTLE 35
TURRET
Boat House
Broomlee Lough
TURRET 35B
Dove Crag
A Pennine Journey
HADRIAN'S WALL (course of)
Enclosure
VALLUM
Common
King's Wicket
Hadrian's Wall Path
Sheepfold
MILECASTLE 36
King's Hill
Kennel Crags
Clew Hill
TURRET 36A
Housesteads
VERCOVICIVM ROMAN FORT
ROMAN WELL
VALLUM
Moss Kennels
Knag Burn
New Beggarbog
Shafts (dis)
Grindon Mill Hills
Chapel Hill
ROMAN WELL
CULTIVATION TERRACES
Information Centre
PC
Tumulus
Beggar Bog
Knag Burn
Sheepfold
Deafley Rigg
Mound
Knag Burn
Little Shield
Tumulus
Grindon Lough
Green Brae
East Crindledykes
Shaft (dis)
East Morwood
West Morwood
Blackdyke Plantation

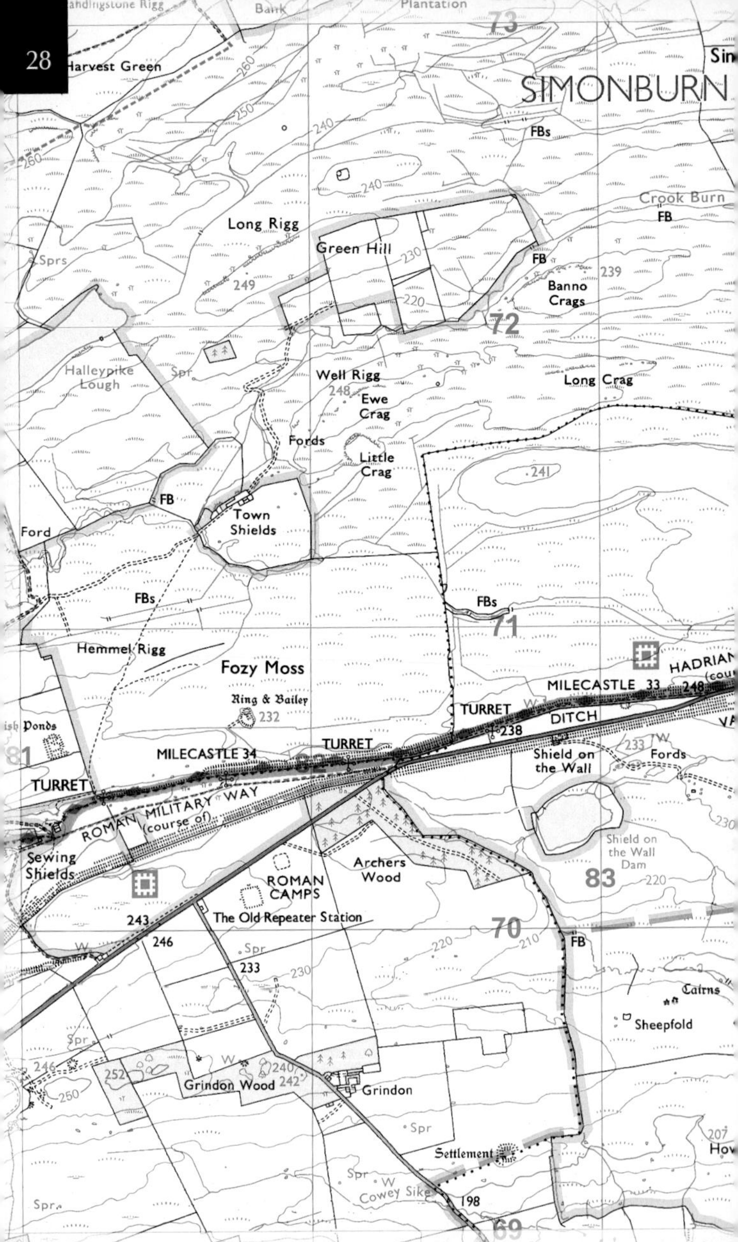
Harvest Green
Bank
Plantation
SIMONBURN
FBs
Crook Burn
FB
Long Rigg
Green Hill
Sprs
249
240
230
220
FB
Banno
Crags
239
Halleypike
Lough
Spr
Well Rigg
248
Ewe
Crag
Long Crag
Fords
Little
Crag
241
FB
Town
Shields
Ford
FBs
FBs
Hemmel Rigg
Fozy Moss
Ring & Bailey
232
HADRIAN
MILECASTLE 33
248
TURRET
238
DITCH
Shield on
the Wall
Fords
233
MILECASTLE 34
TURRET
TURRET
MILITARY WAY
ROMAN
(course of)
Sewing
Shields
ROMAN
CAMPS
Archers
Wood
Shield on
the Wall
Dam
230
220
243
The Old Repeater Station
246
Spr
233
FB
Cairns
Sheepfold
Spr
246
252
Grindon Wood
240
242
Grindon
250
Spr
Settlement
Spr
Cowey Sike
198
207
Spr

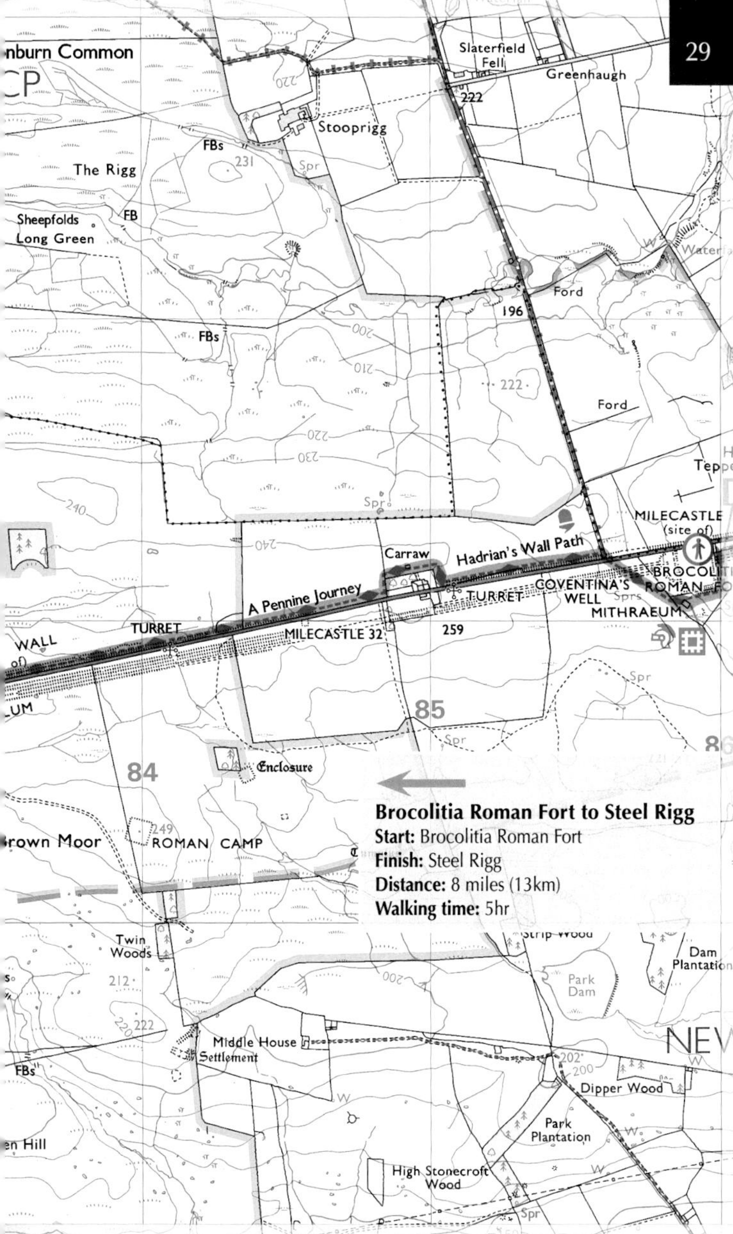

Brocolitia Roman Fort to Steel Rigg

Start: Brocolitia Roman Fort
Finish: Steel Rigg
Distance: 8 miles (13km)
Walking time: 5hr

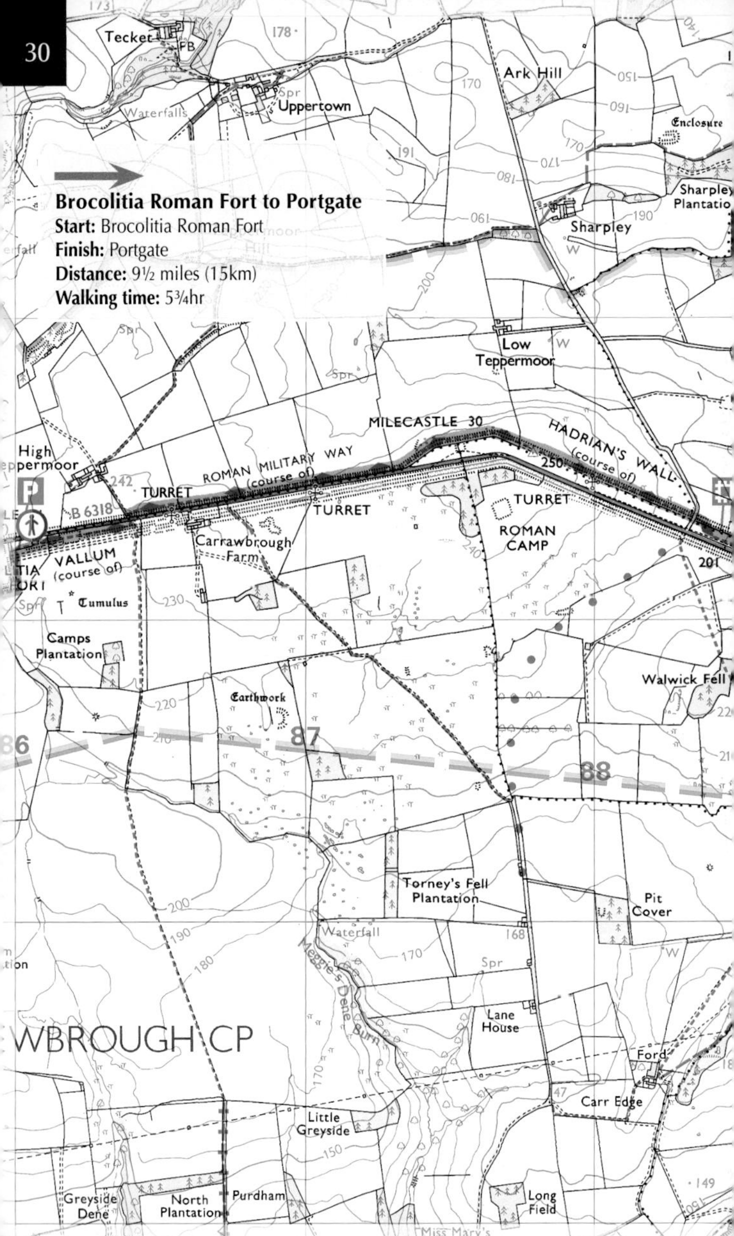

Brocolitia Roman Fort to Portgate
Start: Brocolitia Roman Fort
Finish: Portgate
Distance: 9½ miles (15km)
Walking time: 5¾hr
Tecket
FB
Uppertown
Waterfalls
Ark Hill
Enclosure
Sharpley
Sharpley Plantation
Low Teppermoor
High Teppermoor
MILECASTLE 30
HADRIAN'S WALL (course of)
ROMAN MILITARY WAY (course of)
TURRET
B 6318
Carrawbrough Farm
VALLUM (course of)
Tumulus
Camps Plantation
ROMAN CAMP
Walwick Fell
Earthwork
Torney's Fell Plantation
Pit Cover
Waterfall
Meggie's Dene Burn
Lane House
WBROUGH CP
Ford
Carr Edge
Little Greyside
Greyside Dene
North Plantation
Purdham
Long Field
Miss Mary's

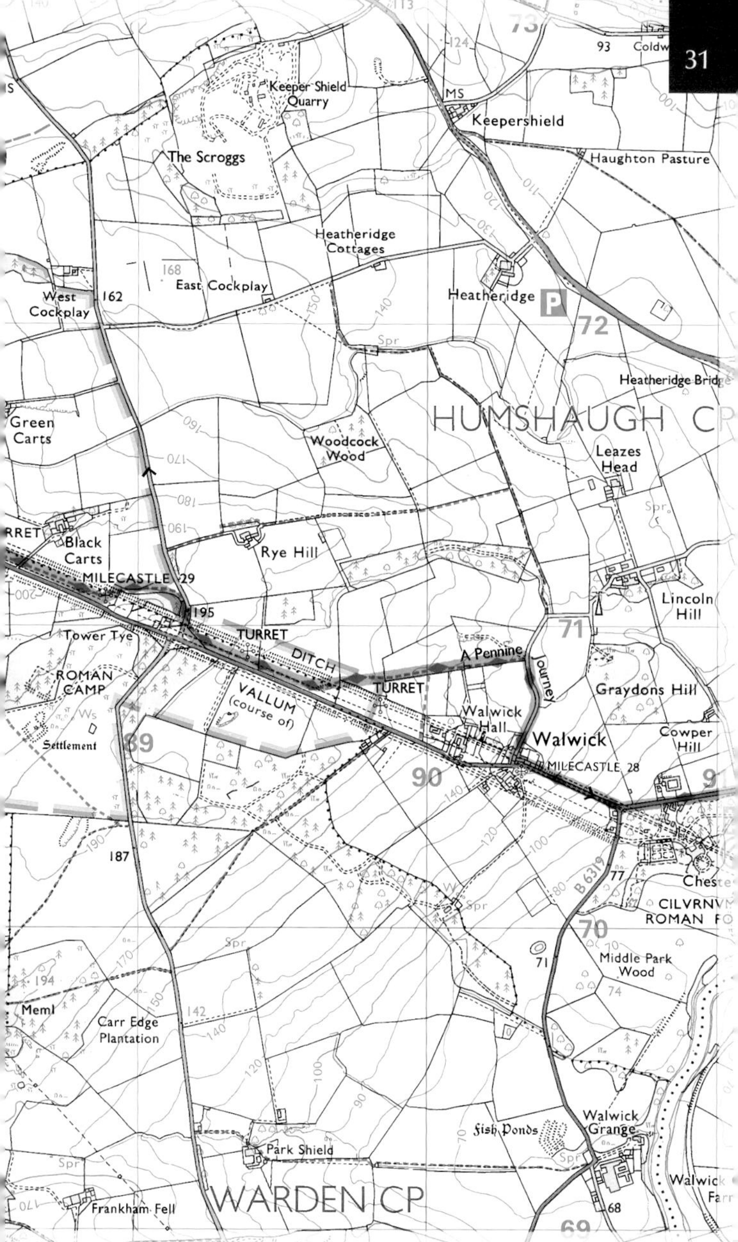
Keeper Shield Quarry
Keepershield
Coldw
Haughton Pasture
The Scroggs
Heatheridge Cottages
East Cockplay
West Cockplay
Heatheridge
Heatheridge Bridge
HUMSHAUGH CP
Green Carts
Woodcock Wood
Leazes Head
Black Carts
Rye Hill
MILECASTLE 29
Lincoln Hill
Tower Tye
TURRET
DITCH
A Pennine Journey
ROMAN CAMP
VALLUM (course of)
TURRET
Graydons Hill
Walwick Hall
Walwick
Cowper Hill
Settlement
MILECASTLE 28
Chesters
CILVRNVM ROMAN FO
Middle Park Wood
Meml
Carr Edge Plantation
Walwick Grange
Fish Ponds
Park Shield
Walwick Farm
Frankham Fell
WARDEN CP

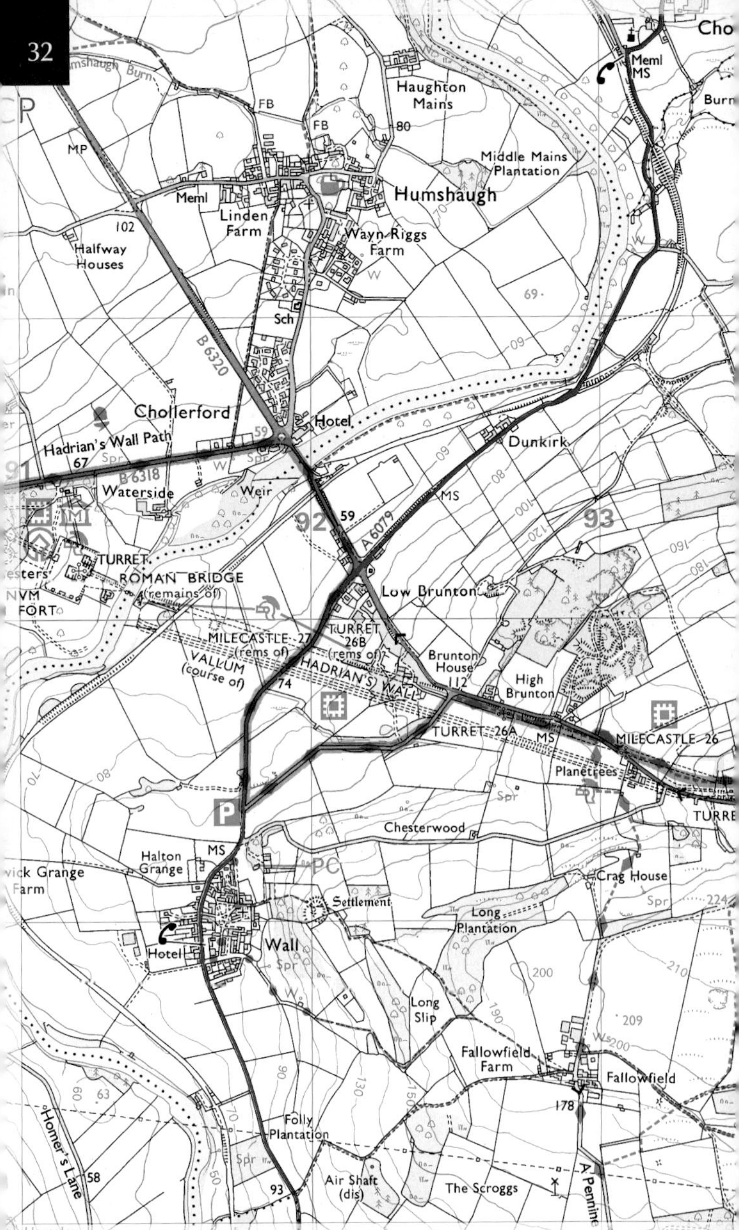
Humshaugh
Haughton Mains
Middle Mains Plantation
Linden Farm
Wayn Riggs Farm
Halfway Houses
Meml
Sch
Chollerford
Hadrian's Wall Path
Hotel
B 6320
B 6318
A 6079
Waterside
Weir
Dunkirk
TURRET
ROMAN BRIDGE (remains of)
Low Brunton
MILECASTLE 27 (rems of)
TURRET 26B (rems of)
VALLUM (course of)
HADRIAN'S WALL
Brunton House
High Brunton
TURRET 26A
MILECASTLE 26
Planetrees
Chesterwood
Halton Grange
Crag House
Settlement
Long Plantation
Wall
Hotel
Long Slip
Fallowfield Farm
Fallowfield
Folly Plantation
Air Shaft (dis)
The Scroggs
Homer's Lane
A Pennine
Horseley
NVM FORT
Cho
Burn

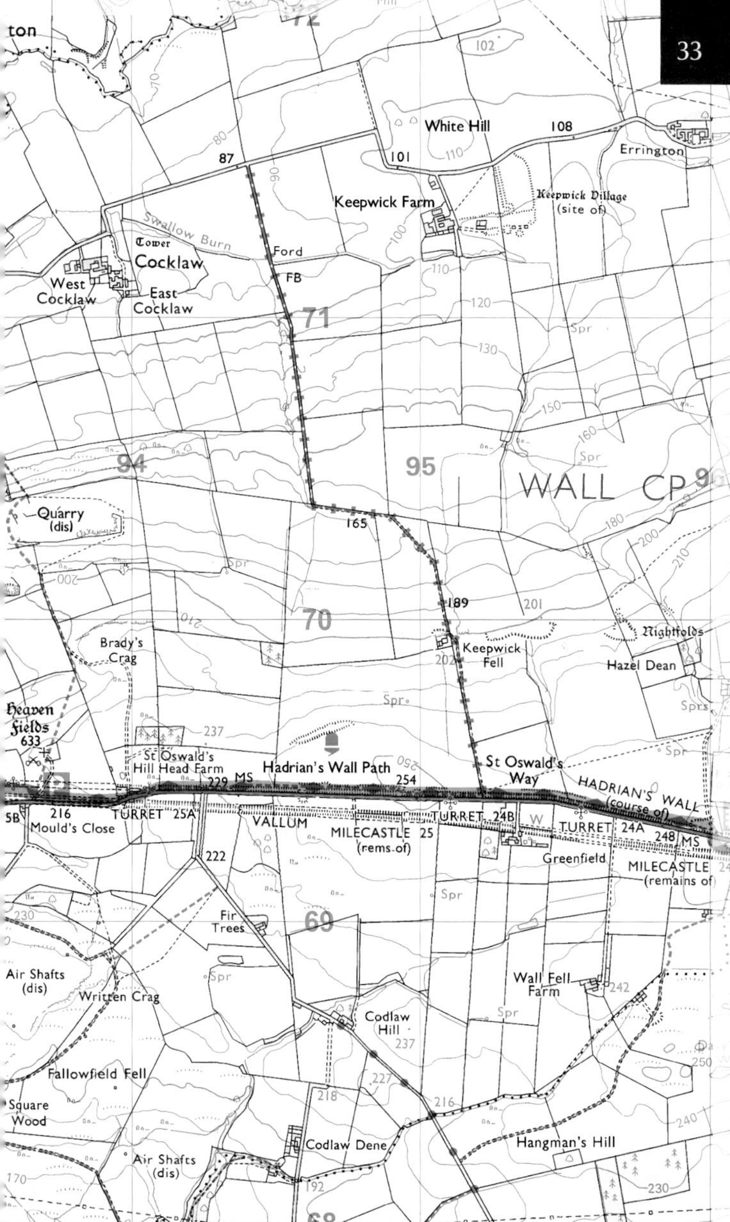

White Hill
108
Errington
87
101
Keepwick Farm
Keepwick Village (site of)
Swallow Burn
Tower
Cocklaw
Ford
FB
West Cocklaw
East Cocklaw
WALL CP
Quarry (dis)
165
189
Keepwick Fell
Nightfolds
Hazel Dean
Brady's Crag
Heaven Fields
633
St Oswald's Hill Head Farm
229 MS
Hadrian's Wall Path
254
St Oswald's Way
HADRIAN'S WALL (course of)
216
Mould's Close
TURRET 25A
VALLUM
MILECASTLE 25 (rems of)
TURRET 24B
TURRET 24A
248 MS
Greenfield
MILECASTLE (remains of)
222
Fir Trees
Air Shafts (dis)
Written Crag
Wall Fell Farm
Codlaw Hill
237
Fallowfield Fell
Square Wood
Codlaw Dene
Hangman's Hill
Air Shafts (dis)

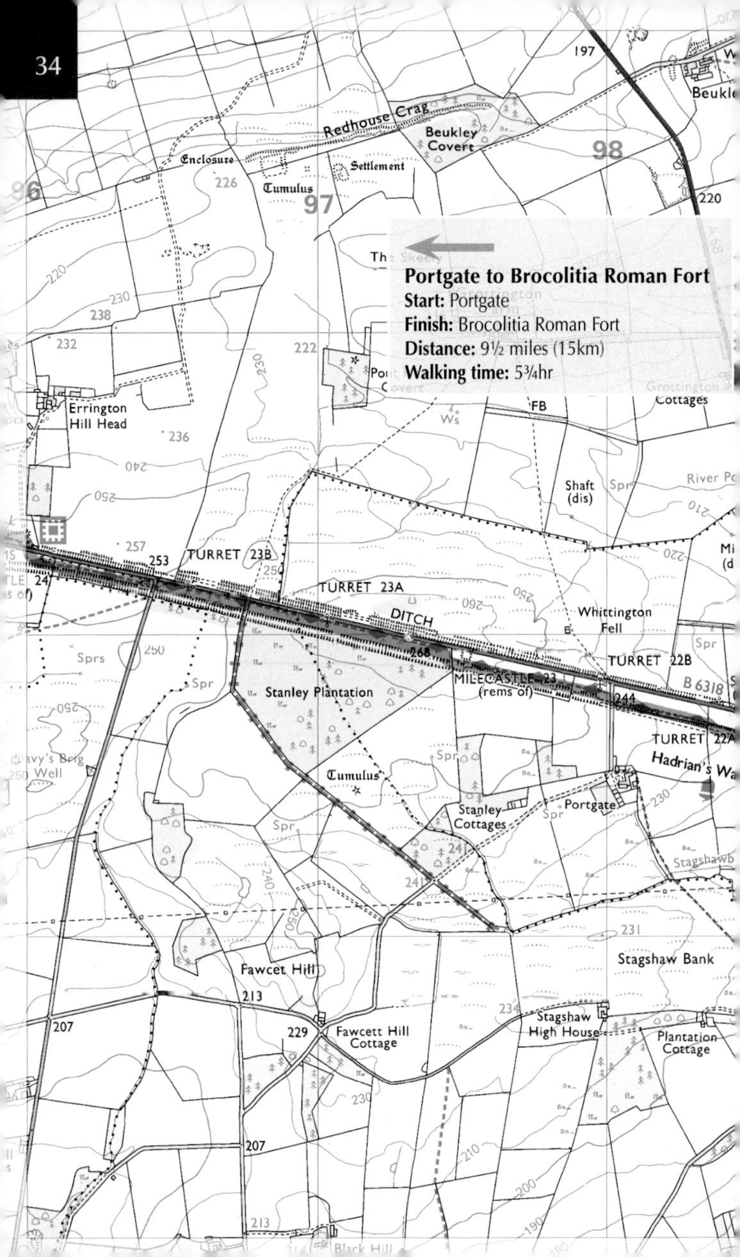

Portgate to Brocolitia Roman Fort

Start: Portgate
Finish: Brocolitia Roman Fort
Distance: 9½ miles (15km)
Walking time: 5¾hr

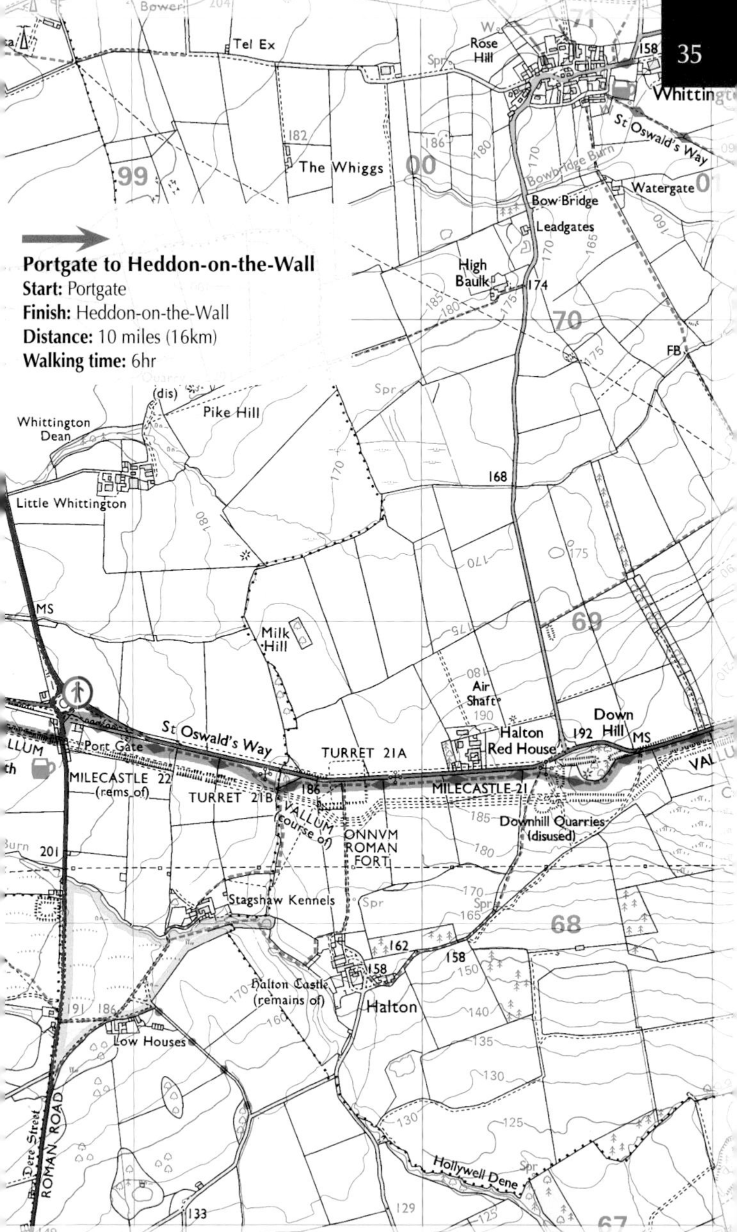

Portgate to Heddon-on-the-Wall
Start: Portgate
Finish: Heddon-on-the-Wall
Distance: 10 miles (16km)
Walking time: 6hr
Bower
Tel Ex
Rose Hill
Whittington
St Oswald's Way
The Whiggs
Bowbridge Burn
Bow Bridge
Watergate
Leadgates
High Baulk
Pike Hill
Whittington Dean
Little Whittington
Milk Hill
Air Shaft
Halton Red House
Down Hill
Port Gate
MILECASTLE 22 (rems of)
TURRET 21B
TURRET 21A
MILECASTLE 21
VALLUM (course of)
ONNVM ROMAN FORT
Downhill Quarries (disused)
Stagshaw Kennels
Halton Castle (remains of)
Halton
Low Houses
Hollywell Dene
ROMAN ROAD
Dere Street

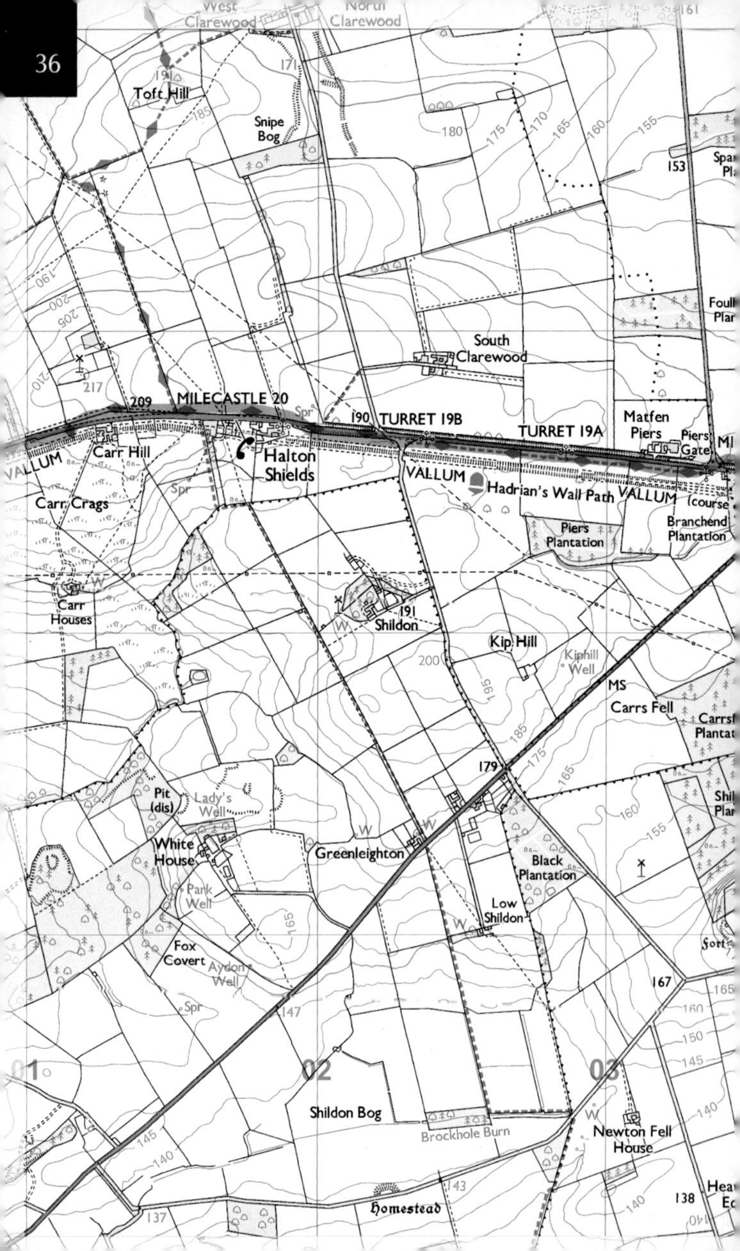

West Clarewood
North Clarewood
Toft Hill
Snipe Bog
South Clarewood
MILECASTLE 20
TURRET 19B
TURRET 19A
Matfen Piers
Piers Gate
Carr Hill
Halton Shields
VALLUM
Hadrian's Wall Path
Carr Crags
Piers Plantation
Branchend Plantation
Carr Houses
Shildon
Kip Hill
Kiphill Well
MS
Carrs Fell
Pit (dis)
Lady's Well
White House
Greenleighton
Black Plantation
Park Well
Low Shildon
Fox Covert
Aydon Well
Shildon Bog
Brockhole Burn
Newton Fell House
Homestead

Butcher Hill
70
148
West Moorhouses
High House Cottages
134
High House
150
145
Becks Plantation
Sparrow Letch
Ford
140
135
East Moorhouses
130
125
146
High House Plantation
69
Angus's Covert
Welton Burn
ASTLE 19
ITCH
Spr
Wall Houses
TURRET 18A
154
MS
TURRET 18B
VALLUM
MILECASTLE 18
Vallum Farm
East Wallhouses
133
MS
TURRET 17A
TURRET 17B
68
130
Whittle Burn
Welton
126
Welton Farm
139
Laker Hall
Shildonhill
67
Hollywell Burn
Cobbler's Lane
155
150
145
140
135
130
125
120
115
114
04
05
06
Well House Farm
127
66

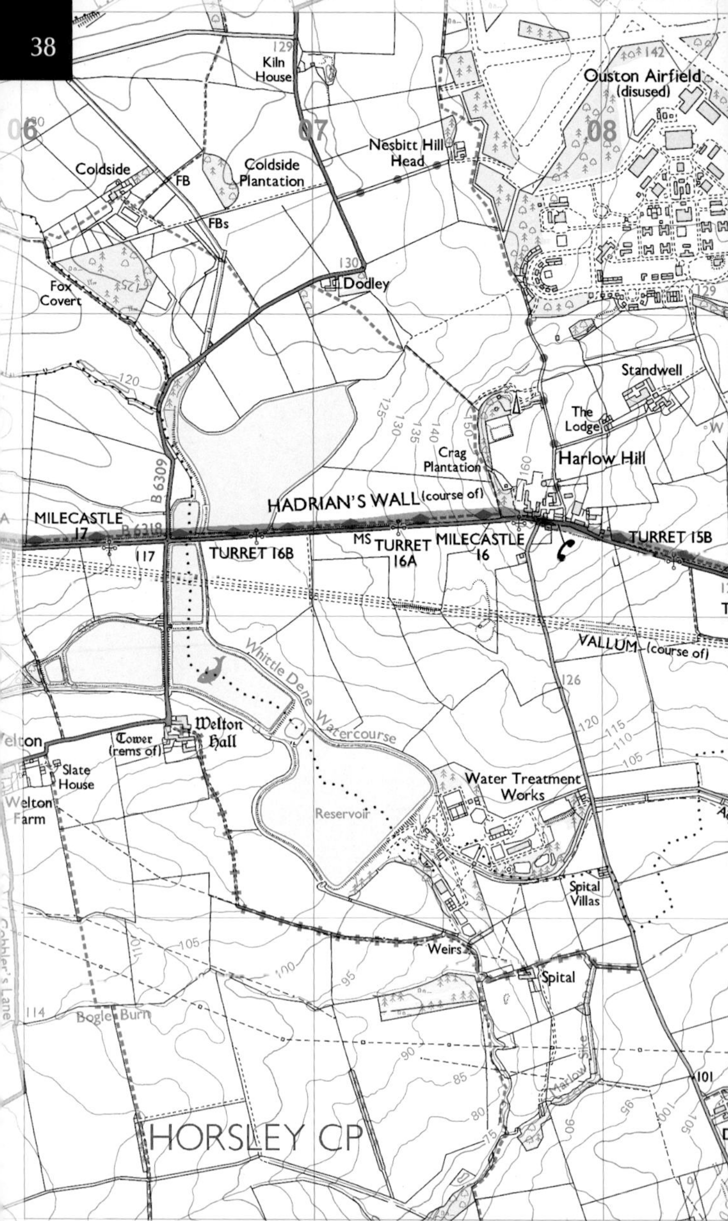
06
07
08
129
Kiln House
Ouston Airfield (disused)
142
Nesbitt Hill Head
Coldside
Coldside Plantation
FB
FBs
Fox Covert
125
130
Dodley
129
120
Standwell
The Lodge
Harlow Hill
Crag Plantation
125
130
135
140
150
160
B 6309
HADRIAN'S WALL (course of)
MILECASTLE 17
B 6318
117
TURRET 16B
MS
TURRET 16A
MILECASTLE 16
TURRET 15B
VALLUM (course of)
Whittle Dene Watercourse
126
120
115
110
105
Welton
Tower (rems of)
Welton Hall
Slate House
Welton Farm
Reservoir
Water Treatment Works
Spital Villas
Weirs
Spital
105
110
100
95
114
Bogle Burn
Cobbler's Lane
90
85
80
75
Marlow Sike
101
HORSLEY CP

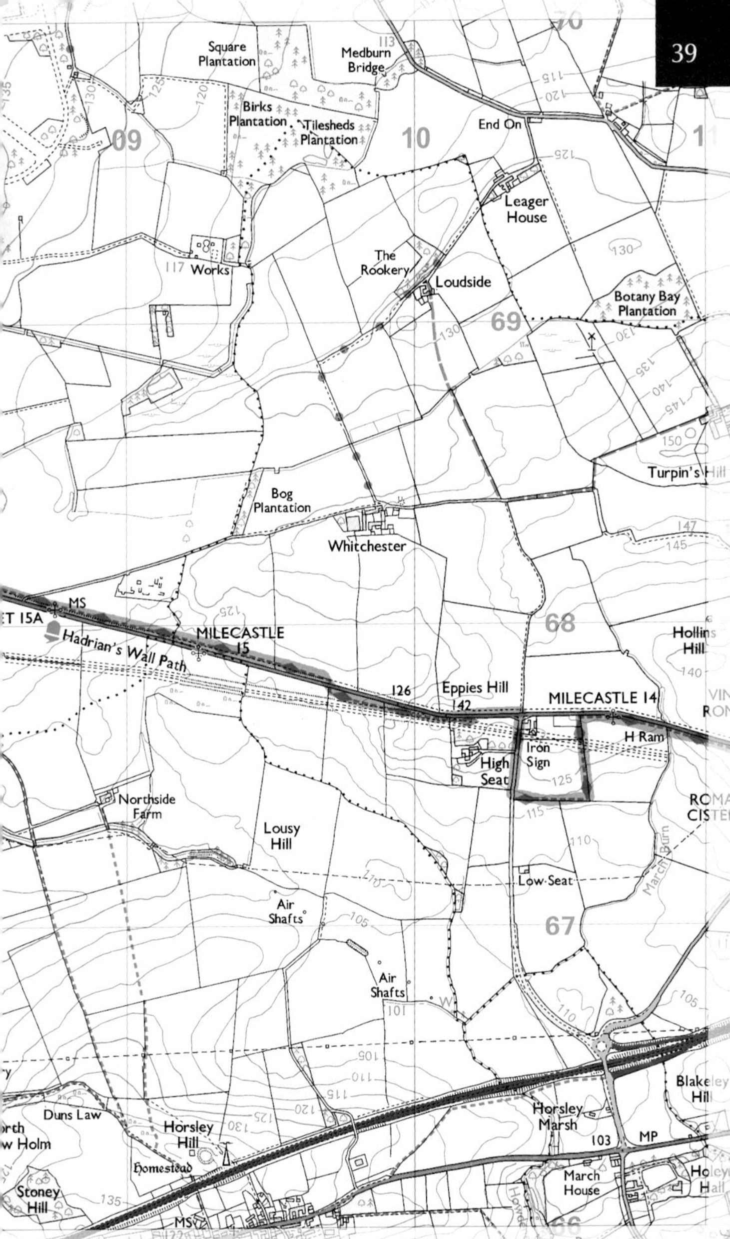
Square Plantation
Medburn Bridge
Birks Plantation
Tilesheds Plantation
End On
09
10
Leager House
Works
The Rookery
Loudside
Botany Bay Plantation
69
Turpin's Hill
Bog Plantation
Whitchester
MS
MILECASTLE 15
Hadrian's Wall Path
68
Hollins Hill
126
Eppies Hill 142
MILECASTLE 14
H Ram
Iron Sign
High Seat
Northside Farm
Lousy Hill
Low Seat
March Burn
Air Shafts
Air Shafts
67
Blakeley Hill
Duns Law
Horsley Hill
Horsley Marsh
103
MP
Homestead
March House
Stoney Hill
MS

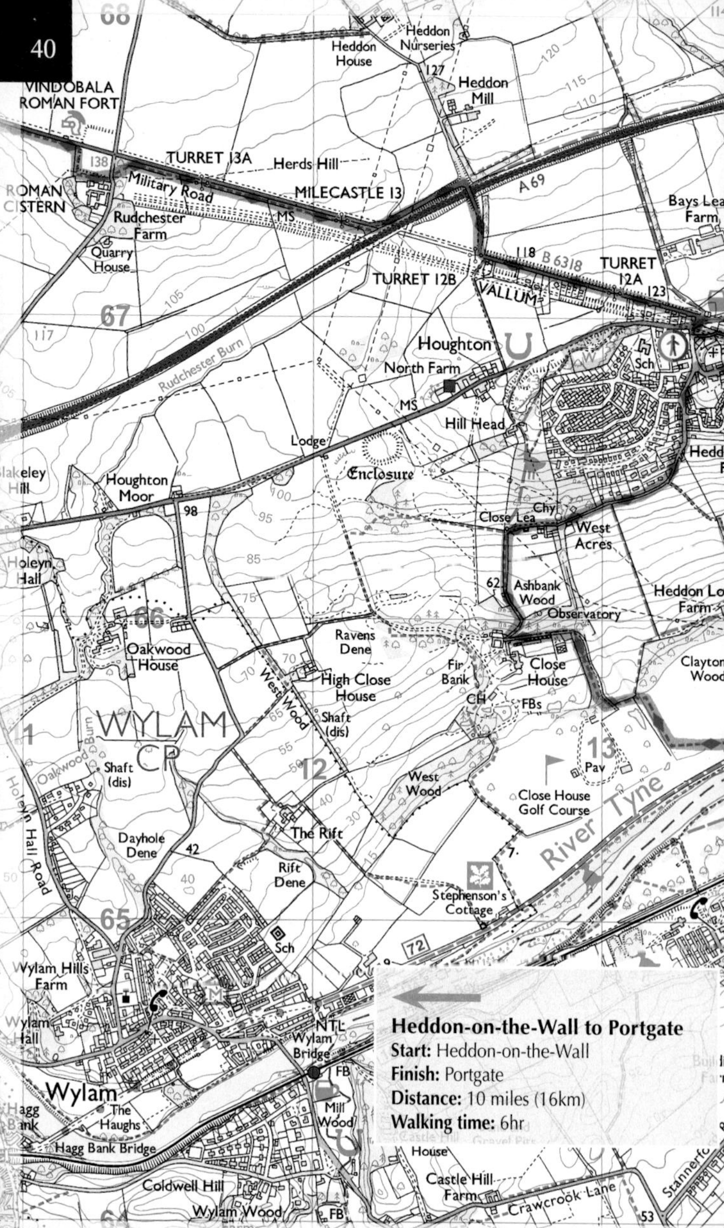
Heddon-on-the-Wall to Portgate
Start: Heddon-on-the-Wall
Finish: Portgate
Distance: 10 miles (16km)
Walking time: 6hr
VINDOBALA ROMAN FORT
ROMAN CISTERN
Rudchester Farm
Quarry House
TURRET 13A
Herds Hill
Military Road
MILECASTLE 13
TURRET 12B
TURRET 12A
VALLUM
Heddon House
Heddon Nurseries
Heddon Mill
A 69
B 6318
Bays Leas Farm
Houghton
North Farm
Hill Head
Rudchester Burn
Lodge
Enclosure
Blakeley Hill
Houghton Moor
Holeyn Hall
Oakwood House
Close Lea
West Acres
Ashbank Wood
Observatory
Heddon Low Farm
Ravens Dene
High Close House
West Wood
Fir Bank
Close House
FBs
Clayton Wood
Shaft (dis)
WYLAM CP
Oakwood Burn
Holeyn Hall Road
Dayhole Dene
The Rift
Rift Dene
West Wood
Pav
Close House Golf Course
River Tyne
Stephenson's Cottage
Sch
Wylam Hills Farm
Wylam Hall
Wylam
The Haughs
Hagg Bank
Hagg Bank Bridge
NTL
Wylam Bridge
FB
Mill Wood
Coldwell Hill
Wylam Wood
Castle Hill House
Castle Hill Farm
Crawcrook Lane

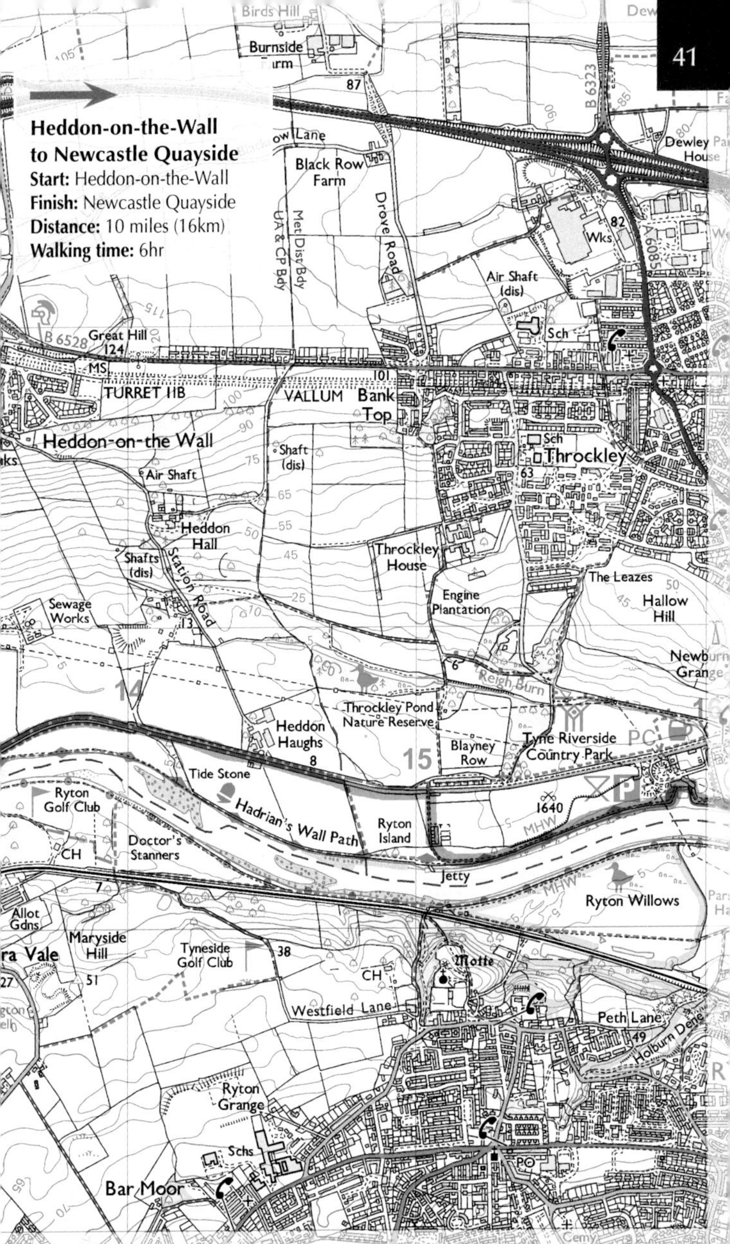
Heddon-on-the-Wall
to Newcastle Quayside
Start: Heddon-on-the-Wall
Finish: Newcastle Quayside
Distance: 10 miles (16km)
Walking time: 6hr
Birds Hill
Burnside Farm
Black Row Farm
Drove Road
Met Dist Bdy
UA & CP Bdy
B 6323
Dewley House
Wks
A 6085
Air Shaft (dis)
Sch
B 6528
Great Hill
MS
TURRET 11B
VALLUM
Bank Top
Heddon-on-the-Wall
Shaft (dis)
Throckley
Air Shaft
Heddon Hall
Shafts (dis)
Station Road
Throckley House
The Leazes
Hallow Hill
Engine Plantation
Sewage Works
Newburn Grange
Reigh Burn
Throckley Pond Nature Reserve
Heddon Haughs
Blayney Row
Tyne Riverside Country Park
PC
Tide Stone
Ryton Golf Club
Hadrian's Wall Path
Ryton Island
1640
MHW
Doctor's Stanners
CH
Jetty
Ryton Willows
Allot Gdns
Maryside Hill
Tyneside Golf Club
Motte
Westfield Lane
Peth Lane
Holburn Dene
Ryton Grange
Schs
Bar Moor
PO
Cemy

Schs
College
17
MILECASTLE 10
(remains of)
Walbottle
Dene
Walbottle
TURRET 9B
Sch
87
HADRIAN'S
WALL
(course of)
Schs
Sch
18
FB
MILECASTLE 9
B 6528
VALLUM
(course of)
Walbottle
Hall
Rye Hill
Newburn
Grange
34
Knop Law
Sch
Newburn
Walbottle Brickworks
Nature Reserve
77
Cemy
72
PO
Parson's
Haugh
Newburn
Bridge
Leming
El
Sub Sta
Ind
Est
17
Ryton Haugh
141
RYTON
Addison
Sand Pit
(disused)
Ind Est
Hedgefield
Hotel
B 6317
Sch
67
18
Cromwell
Newburn
Haugh
Wks
Sch
Stella
Stella Lane
Stella
House
Hexham Old Road
Stargate
Image
Hill
Path Head
Farm
Met Dist Bdy
Opencast
Workings
Pit
(dis)
Weir
A 695
FB
Sch
Bewes Hills
Beweshill Lane
Path
Head
Schs

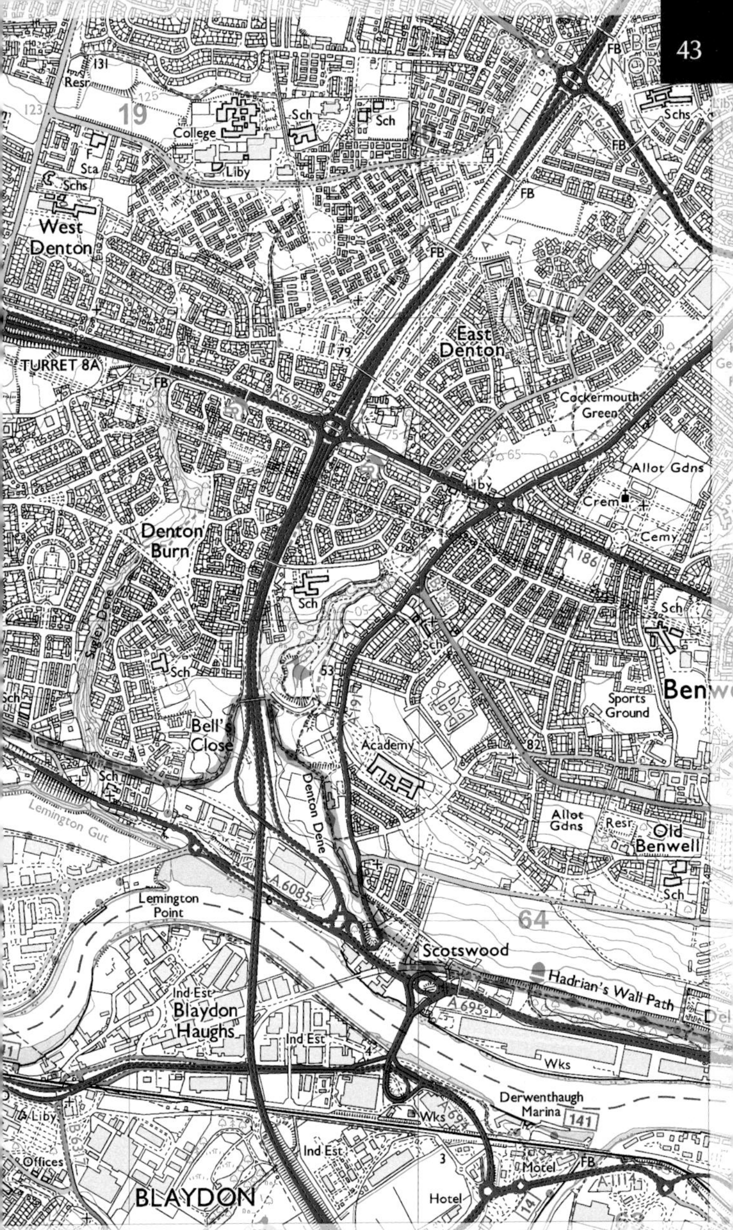
Resr
College
Sch
Sch
Liby
F
Sta
Schs
West
Denton
FB
Schs
East
Denton
TURRET 8A
FB
A 69
Cockermouth
Green
Allot Gdns
Liby
Crem
Cemy
A 186
Denton
Burn
Sch
Sugley Dene
Sch
Sch
Sch
Benwell
Sports
Ground
Bell's
Close
Academy
Denton Dene
Lemington Gut
Sch
Allot
Gdns
Resr
Old
Benwell
Sch
A 6085
Lemington
Point
Scotswood
Hadrian's Wall Path
A 695
Ind Est
Blaydon
Haughs
Ind Est
Wks
Derwenthaugh
Marina
Liby
Wks
Ind Est
Offices
Motel
FB
A 1114
Hotel
BLAYDON
Cemy

Hill
Sch
28
Allot Gdns
Blue House
B1305
Liby
Fenham
Hunter's Moor
Sch
Schs
Coll
Allot Gdns
Schs
Spital Tongues
Sch
Cemy
Playing Field
College
enwell
TEMPLE
Sch
Sch
Arthur's Hill
HADRIAN'S WALL (course of)
F Sta
Sch
Sch
Pol Sta
Sch
B1305
Sch
Liby
PO
MOSQUE
Sch
Sch
South Benwell
Sch
Cemy
Delaval
Paradise
Wks
Elswick
Sch
Lib
Jetty
Wharf
Jetty
Gateshead Metro Centre Sta
72
Hadrian
14
Met Dist Bdy
Wks
The Metrocentre
Sch
Wks
Cross Lane Meadows Nature Reserve
27
Dunston
BMX
Sch

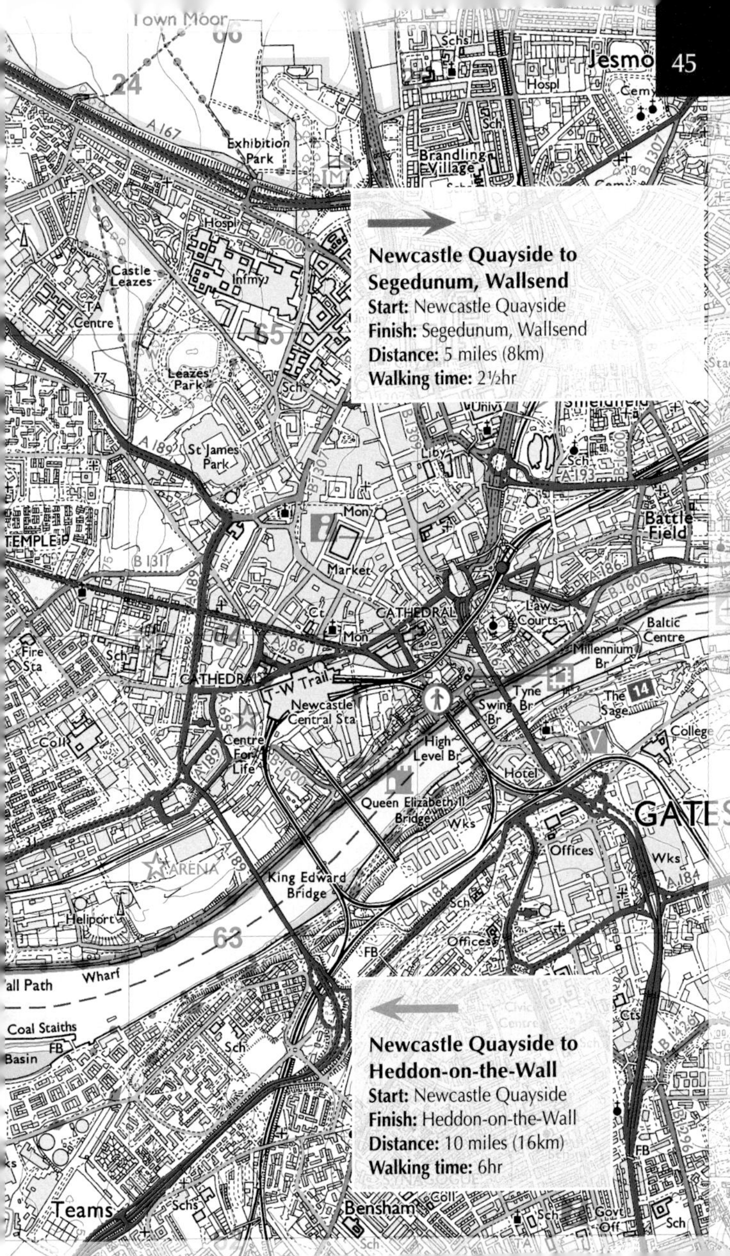

Newcastle Quayside to Segedunum, Wallsend
Start: Newcastle Quayside
Finish: Segedunum, Wallsend
Distance: 5 miles (8km)
Walking time: 2½hr

Newcastle Quayside to Heddon-on-the-Wall
Start: Newcastle Quayside
Finish: Heddon-on-the-Wall
Distance: 10 miles (16km)
Walking time: 6hr

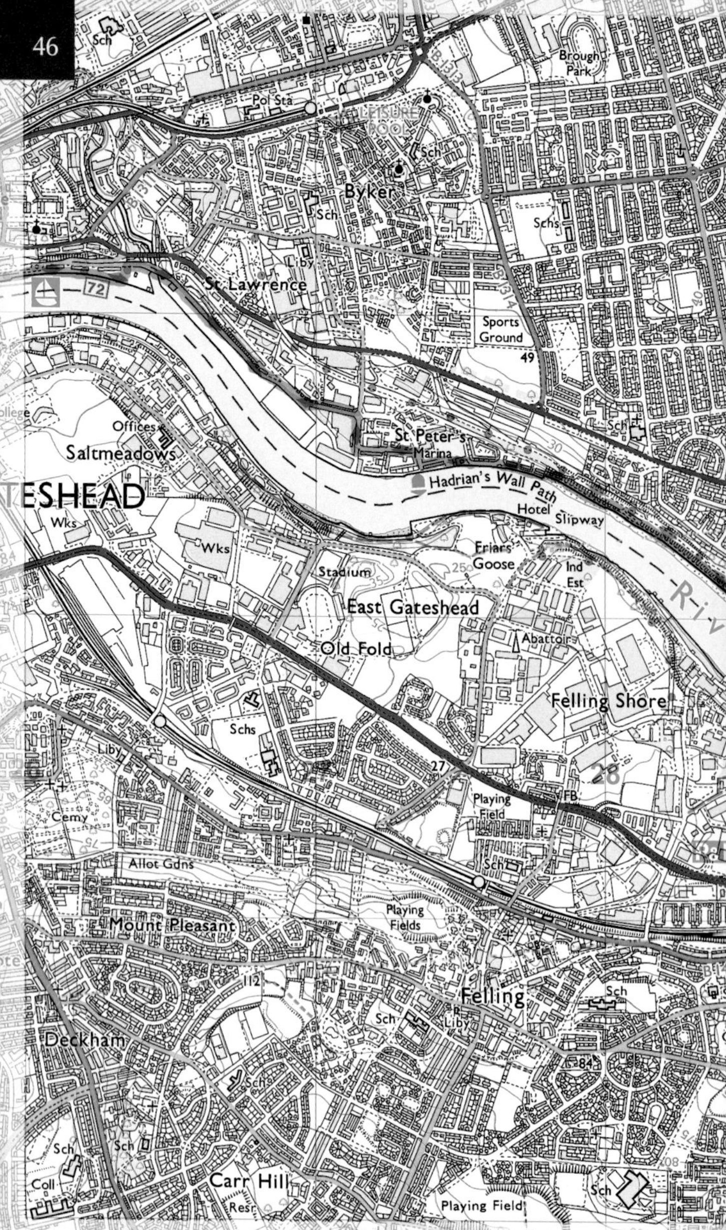
Sch
Brough Park
B1313
Pol Sta
LEISURE POOL
Sch
Byker
Sch
Schs
Liby
St Lawrence
B1314
72
Sports Ground
49
Sch
St Peter's Marina
Offices
Saltmeadows
Hadrian's Wall Path
TESHEAD
Hotel
Slipway
Wks
Wks
Friars Goose
Ind Est
Stadium
East Gateshead
Abattoir
Old Fold
Felling Shore
Schs
Liby
27
28
Cemy
Playing Field
FB
Allot Gdns
Sch
Playing Fields
Mount Pleasant
112
Felling
Sch
Sch
Liby
Deckham
84
Sch
Sch
Sch
Coll
Carr Hill
Resr
Playing Field
Sch

Low Walker
B1313
Sch
Job Cen
Liby
School
Walker
TA Centre
Wks
Met Dist Bdy
Wincomblee
Wharf
Wks
Wharves
Pelaw Main
Sch
PO
72
Sch
Anthony's
Walker Riverside Park
t Anthony's Point
Tyne
14
Wks
Bill Quay Farm
Bill Quay
Playing Fields
29
Sch
Pelaw
A185
FB
Cemy
Heworth
Sch
Schs
58
Playing Field
Schs
Hebburn New Town
B1297
Liby
64
Sports Ground
Cemy
Wks
Schs
F Sta
47
63
College
School
Sch
Monkton Mill Farm
55
50
62
South Wardley Farm
Met Dist Bdy
Wardley
M195
A184
White Mare Pool
B1288
A194(M)
Sch
61

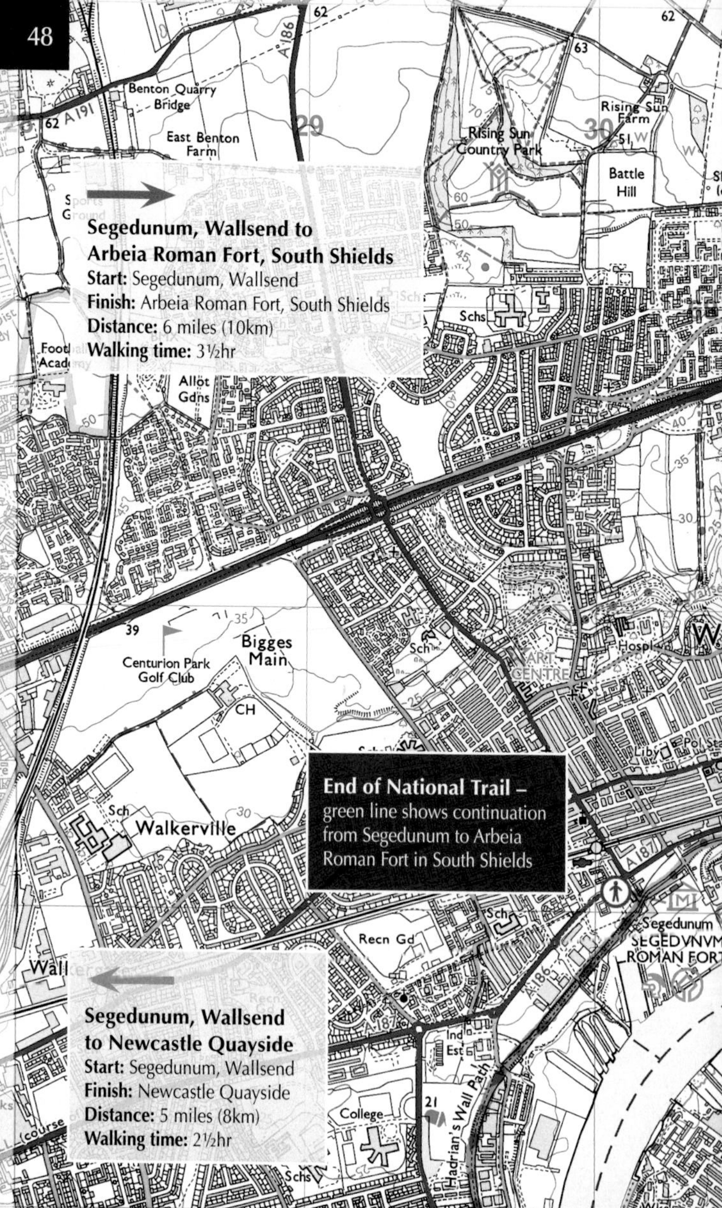

Segedunum, Wallsend to Arbeia Roman Fort, South Shields
Start: Segedunum, Wallsend
Finish: Arbeia Roman Fort, South Shields
Distance: 6 miles (10km)
Walking time: 3½hr

End of National Trail – green line shows continuation from Segedunum to Arbeia Roman Fort in South Shields

Segedunum, Wallsend to Newcastle Quayside
Start: Segedunum, Wallsend
Finish: Newcastle Quayside
Distance: 5 miles (8km)
Walking time: 2½hr

Willington Farm
Pol HQ
Hotel
North Tyneside Steam Railway
Bluehouse Bridges
A1058
West Chirton
Trading Estate
Sch
Willington Square
Coll
Liby
Playing Fields
Playing Fields
Coll
Schs
Willington
Cemy
Howdon
Sch
Holy Cross
B1315
Burn Closes
War Meml
Liby
SEND
College
NTL
Rosehill
Sch
Wks
Gas Works
Cemy
Sch
Willington Gut
FB
72
Sta
Point Pleasant
A187
Toll
Toll
Willington Quay
Wks
Wks
Jarrow Staith
Jetty
Wks
Hebburn Colliery
72
14
TH
Sch
Schs
Liby
B1297

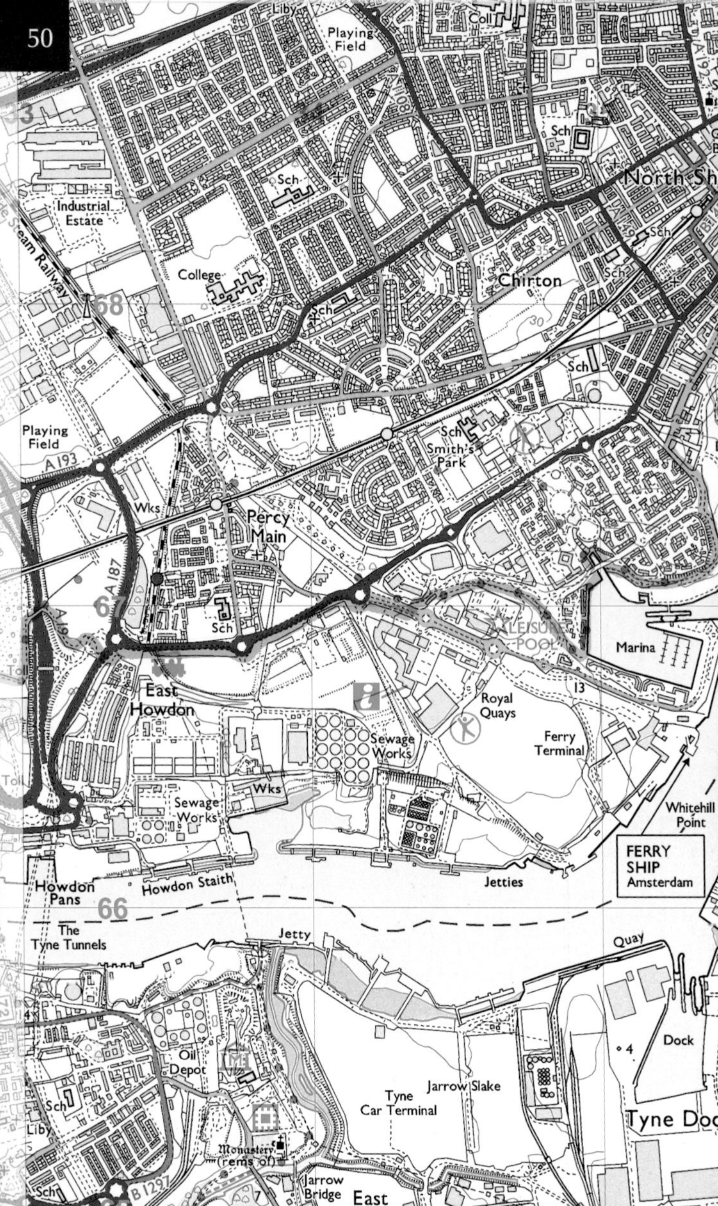

Liby
Playing Field
Coll
North Shi
Sch
Industrial Estate
College
Chirton
Playing Field
A 193
Wks
Percy Main
Smith's Park
A 187
East Howdon
Marina
Royal Quays
Ferry Terminal
Sewage Works
Wks
Sewage Works
Whitehill Point
FERRY SHIP Amsterdam
Howdon Pans
Howdon Staith
Jetties
The Tyne Tunnels
Jetty
Quay
Oil Depot
Dock
Tyne Car Terminal
Jarrow Slake
Tyne Doc
Monastery (rems of)
Jarrow Bridge
East
Liby
B 1297

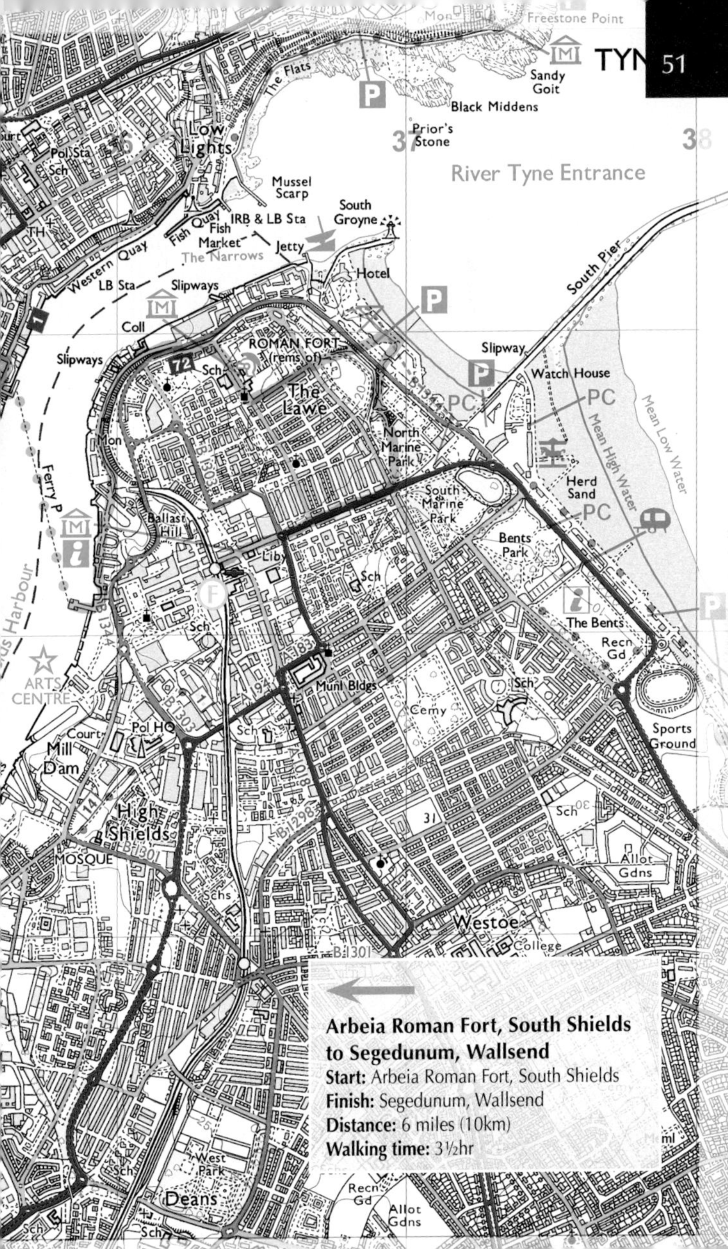
Freestone Point
TYN
Sandy Goit
Black Middens
Prior's Stone
37
38
River Tyne Entrance
The Flats
Low Lights
Pol Sta
Sch
TH
Mussel Scarp
South Groyne
IRB & LB Sta
Fish Quay
Fish Market
The Narrows
Jetty
Western Quay
LB Sta
Slipways
Hotel
South Pier
Coll
Slipways
ROMAN FORT (rems of)
72
Sch
The Lawe
Slipway
Watch House
PC
Mean High Water
Mean Low Water
North Marine Park
Mon
Ferry P
B1303
Herd Sand
South Marine Park
Ballast Hill
Bents Park
Liby
Sch
The Bents
Recn Gd
Harbour
B1344
Sch
A183
Munl Bldgs
ARTS CENTRE
Cemy
Sch
Sports Ground
Court
Mill Dam
Pol HQ
Sch
A1018
High Shields
B1298
Sch
31
MOSQUE
B1301
Allot Gdns
Schs
Westoe
College
B1301
Sch
West Park
Deans
Recn Gd
Allot Gdns
Sch
Arbeia Roman Fort, South Shields to Segedunum, Wallsend
Start: Arbeia Roman Fort, South Shields
Finish: Segedunum, Wallsend
Distance: 6 miles (10km)
Walking time: 3½hr

LEGEND OF SYMBOLS USED ON ORDNANCE SURVEY 1:25,000 (EXPLORER) MAPPING

ROADS AND PATHS — Not necessarily rights of way

M1 or A6(M) — Motorway — Service Area — 7 Junction Number

A 35 — Dual carriageway — Service Area — T1 Toll road junction

A30 — Main road

B 3074 — Secondary road

Narrow road with passing places

Road under construction

Road generally more than 4 m wide

Road generally less than 4 m wide

Other road, drive or track, fenced and unfenced

Gradient: steeper than 20% (1 in 5); 14% (1 in 7) to 20% (1 in 5)

Ferry — Ferry; Ferry P – passenger only

Path

RAILWAYS

Multiple track, Single track — standard gauge

Narrow gauge or Light rapid transit system (LRTS) and station

Road over; road under; level crossing

Cutting; tunnel; embankment

Station, open to passengers; siding

PUBLIC RIGHTS OF WAY

Footpath

Bridleway

Byway open to all traffic

Restricted byway

The representation on this map of any other road, track or path is no evidence of the existence of a right of way

ARCHAEOLOGICAL AND HISTORICAL INFORMATION

Site of antiquity — VILLA Roman — Visible earthwork

1066 Site of battle (with date) — Castle Non-Roman

Information provided by English Heritage for England and the Royal Commissions on the Ancient and Historical Monuments for Scotland and Wales

OTHER PUBLIC ACCESS

• • •	Other routes with public access	The exact nature of the rights on these routes and the existence of any restrictions may be checked with the local highway authority. Alignments are based on the best information available
◆ ◆ ◆	Recreational route	
◆ ◆ ◆	National Trail	Long Distance Route
- - - - - - - - - - -	Permissive footpath	Footpaths and bridleways along which landowners have permitted public use but which are not rights of way. The agreement may be withdrawn
— — — — —	Permissive bridleway	
• • •	Traffic-free cycle route	
1 **1**	National cycle network	route number – traffic free; on road

ACCESS LAND

Firing and test ranges in the area. Danger! Observe warning notices

Access permitted within managed controls, for example, local byelaws. Visit **www.access.mod.uk** for information

England and Wales

Access land boundary and tint

Access land in wooded area

Access information point

Portrayal of access land on this map is intended as a guide to land which is normally available for access on foot, for example access land created under the Countryside and Rights of Way Act 2000, and land managed by the National Trust, Forestry Commission and Woodland Trust. Access for other activities may also exist. Some restrictions will apply; some land will be excluded from open access rights. The depiction of rights of access does not imply or express any warranty as to its accuracy or completeness. Observe local signs and follow the Countryside Code.
Visit **www.countrysideaccess.gov.uk** for up-to-date information

BOUNDARIES

— + — +	National
— · — · —	County (England)
— — — —	Unitary Authority (UA), Metropolitan District (Met Dist), London Borough (LB) or District (Scotland & Wales are solely Unitary Authorities)
· · · · · · · · · · ·	Civil Parish (CP) (England) or Community (C) (Wales)
▬▬ ▬▬	National Park boundary

VEGETATION

Limits of vegetation are defined by positioning of symbols

- Coniferous trees
- Non-coniferous trees
- Coppice
- Orchard
- Scrub
- Bracken, heath or rough grassland
- Marsh, reeds or saltings

HEIGHTS AND NATURAL FEATURES

52 · Ground survey height
284 · Air survey height

Surface heights are to the nearest metre above mean sea level. Where two heights are shown, the first height is to the base of the triangulation pillar and the second (in brackets) to the highest natural point of the hill

Vertical face/cliff

75
60
50

Contours are at 5 or 10 metre vertical intervals

Loose rock | Boulders | Outcrop | Scree

Water

Mud

Sand; sand and shingle

SELECTED TOURIST AND LEISURE INFORMATION

Building of historic interest
Cadw
Heritage centre
Camp site
Caravan site
Camping and caravan site
Castle / fort
Cathedral / Abbey
Craft centre
Country park
Cycle trail
Mountain bike trail
Cycle hire
English Heritage
Fishing
Forestry Commission Visitor centre
Garden / arboretum
Golf course or links
Historic Scotland
Information centre, all year
Information centre, seasonal
Horse riding
Museum
National Park Visitor Centre (park logo) e.g. Yorkshire Dales

Nature reserve
National Trust
Other tourist feature
Parking
Park and ride, all year
Park and ride, seasonal
Picnic site
Preserved railway
PC Public Convenience
Public house/s
Recreation / leisure / sports centre
Roman site (Hadrian's Wall only)
Slipway
Telephone, emergency
Telephone, public
Telephone, roadside assistance
Theme / pleasure park
Viewpoint
Visitor centre
Walks / trails
World Heritage site / area
Water activites
Boat trips
Boat hire

(For complete legend and symbols, see any OS Explorer map).

Hadrian's Wall Path

This map booklet accompanies the latest edition of Mark Richards' guidebook to walking Hadrian's Wall Path National Trail. Described in both directions, the main description is west to east between Bowness-on-Solway and Wallsend, Newcastle, with an extension east to South Shields and a special heritage route through Tyneside from Heddon-on-the-Wall to Segedunum, following the line of the Wall, called Hadrian's Toon Trail. The guidebook features annotated 1:100,000 mapping alongside detailed step-by-step route descriptions and extensive information about this World Heritage Site.

Milecastle 42 at Cawfields Crags

OTHER CICERONE TRAIL GUIDES

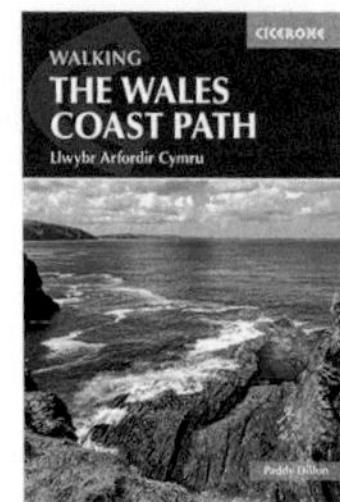

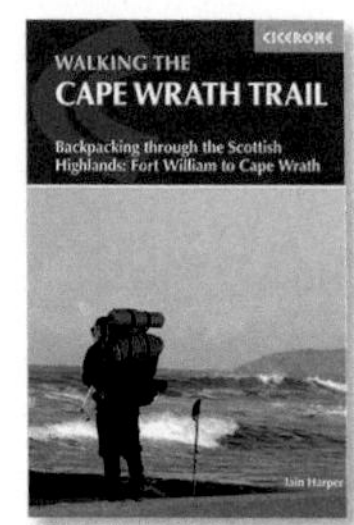

Cicerone National Trails Guides

The South West Coast Path
The South Downs Way
The North Downs Way
The Ridgeway National Trail
The Thames Path
The Cotswold Way
The Peddars Way and
Norfolk Coast Path
The Cleveland Way and
the Yorkshire Wolds Way
Cycling the Pennine Bridleway
The Pennine Way
Hadrian's Wall Path
The Pembrokeshire Coast Path
Offa's Dyke Path
Glyndŵr's Way
The Southern Upland Way
The Speyside Way
The West Highland Way
The Great Glen Way

Visit our website for a full
list of Cicerone Trail Guides
www.cicerone.co.uk